In Praise of *Which Future?*

I0095662

"*In* Which Future?, *David Greene synthesizes principles from evolutionary biology, linguistics, systems engineering, philosophy and political science to argue that if we want any future at all, we don't really have a choice: we must embrace a radical shift in the way we engage with the world and with other human beings. A thoughtful, provocative and important book.*"

Dr. Sally E. Goldin, Carnegie-Mellon University Thailand, Assistant Professor of Computer Engineering

"*David Greene's powerful insight is in showing how the relationships of humans to nature, and humans to other humans, are deeply interconnected, as well as what this implies. We cannot restore our relationship to the natural world if we do not simultaneously restore our relationships with one another, and our commitment to justice and human flourishing.* Which Future?, *aptly described as a work of moral philosophy, offers us a wake-up call well worth heeding.*"

Alan Mallach, Urbanist, Author of *The Divided City*

"*In* Which Future?, *David Greene draws on principles of cognitive science, evolution, and general systems theory to derive a small set of fundamental moral imperatives. This constitutes an insightful and important new approach to moral philosophy, challenging current neoliberal dogma and speaking directly to central issues confronting humanity. A timely and well-written call to action for us all.*"

Mark R. Lepper, Stanford University Professor of Psychology, emeritus

"*I must have read a thousand times someone saying that we need to revise our way of thinking if we're going to avoid climate and human catastrophe. But such comments are always light on just how we should do that. In* Which Future?, *Greene fills that gap with a compelling prescription for philosophical and political change.*"

Robert Adler, Author of *Science Firsts and Medical Firsts*

WHICH FUTURE?

CHOOSING DEMOCRACY, CLIMATE HEALTH, AND **SOCIAL JUSTICE**

DAVID GREENE

NATURAL HUMANIST PRESS
Palo Alto, California

Library of Congress control number: 2022918515

ISBN 979-8-9870-2250-4 (print book)
ISBN 979-8-9870-2251-1 (e-book)

For Jeremy and Jane,

*without whose love and support this book
would never have been written*

CONTENTS

INTRODUCTION

At the core of every moral code there is a picture of human nature, a map of the universe, and a version of history.

– **Walter Lippman (1922)**[1]

I wrote this book in response to an existential threat to humanity: our planetary climate crisis. We know we must act urgently to transform the global economy to minimize carbon emissions. Yet active resistance to change, inertia, and apathy combine to defuse the urgency. So if we are to redirect society toward sustainability before it is too late, we face another critical imperative: to change human *thinking* about our relationship to Earth and to each other.

Which Future? aims to change human thinking, one reader at a time. First, it explains how human reality is socially constructed, so that it is clearly within our power to change our own belief systems. Second, it describes how humanity is interconnected with nature, so that our very survival depends on keeping nature healthy. Third, it presents the full worldview of "natural humanism," which provides a vision of people interconnected with the planet and each other, and committed to everyone's well-being and fulfillment.

Since the advent of Darwin, ecology, and, more recently, cognitive and cultural psychology, we no longer understand ourselves or the world as our nation's founders did. *Which Future?* advances a moral philosophy grounded in 21st-century knowledge of ourselves and our planet. A multi-disciplinary synthesis, the book provides an original, contemporary rationale for the sustainability and social justice goals widely shared by progressive thinkers around the world.

The worldview of natural humanism is built on a few key premises that lead to insights, values, and principles that many people already embrace, but which are ignored or marginalized because they cannot be reconciled with the established neoliberal political regime. This book pulls these pieces together into a coherent moral framework from which I derive the kinds of institutions, policies, and practices needed if humanity is to thrive or even survive the climate crisis. I purposely stop short of prescription, believing that diverse, culturally-specific solutions should emerge from democratic deliberation.

I offer *Which Future?* to readers as a timely and hopeful vision of human potential, and of the scope and depth of the transformation in thinking our species urgently needs to save ourselves from self-destruction.

––––––––

The climate crisis looms over humanity and dwarfs everything else in ultimate importance. Now is a unique, unprecedented moment in history in which our entire species has a clear common interest in avoiding climate catastrophe. Such a superordinate threat should bring the global community together, and it would, if only we all perceived it the same way. Alas, we do not. The reality of climate change is too immense, complex, and abstract for most people to grasp. It is both an immediate threat and a long-term catastrophe in the making. It implicates our entire way of life, overwhelming attempts to simplify the issues. For these reasons among others, most Americans are either ignorant, apathetic, or hopeless, or they are in denial about it.

I first became aware of global warming in the 1980s, when it was still called the "greenhouse effect." As years passed, it became increasingly apparent that the fossil fuel industry was actively sowing disinformation to create confusion about climate change, thereby suppressing political momentum to respond appropriately. Over the decades, worldwide carbon emissions continued to increase dramatically, while escalating predictions of dire consequences from the global science community appeared to fall on deaf ears.[2] Then, in 2018, a devastating report from the United Nations International Panel on Climate Change stated the overwhelming scientific consensus that the world had only about one decade left to utterly transform its energy systems or risk catastrophic ecological and social disaster.[3] In response, in 2019, mainstream journalists finally began describing the reality of the situation as the climate *crisis*, and during the 2020 U.S. election campaigns, for the first time, some candidates referred to climate change as "an existential threat to humanity."

Helping to guide our species toward an ecologically sustainable way of life is the first focus and goal of *Which Future?*. The second focus and goal is to accelerate progress toward justice, meant in its broadest sense to encompass the general principles of inclusion, equality, fair distribution of resources, due process, and freedom from coercion—principles that beg to be embedded in the specific contexts of racial, economic, and climate justice. The twin goals of sustainability and social justice are joined together not only in the practical sense that we cannot achieve one without the other, but also in the existential sense that both goals are rooted in relationships of interconnection and interdependence. In *Which Future?* I examine these principles and the moral issues they raise through the lens of *humanism*; specifically, the humanist foundational imperative to promote and celebrate the health, well-being, and fulfillment of *all* human beings. Sustainability and justice are the intertwined and complementary lodestars toward which this moral compass points.[4]

A New Moral Compass

This century's climate crisis and glut of injustice are consequences of longstanding institutions, laws, policies, and practices of industrial civilization which will be very costly and painful to change. Moreover, and importantly, these institutions and practices are justified by conventional beliefs that give them the patina of normality and inevitability. Some of these beliefs have long histories, tracing their roots to great minds of the 17th and 18th centuries such as John Locke and Adam Smith, whose ideas are still referenced in daily opinion pieces. Authority figures routinely validate and reinforce the status quo in terms that are essentially baked into the culture. The popular word for this established regime is "neoliberalism," which I use often in this book to refer to the political economy strongly favoring privatization of public resources and minimal government regulation that, in its current iteration, dates back to the start of the Reagan administration four decades ago.[5] Mainstream media are devoted to legitimating established thinking or questioning it only within narrowly drawn boundaries. Problems are defined and new challenges are described using familiar terms and received wisdom. In all these ways conventional storytelling and beliefs serve to actively resist change. This conservative, inertial tendency is antithetical to an urgency to transform our way of life.

If urgency is required and conventional beliefs actively resist change in the face of new perils, the need for a new moral vision seems obvious. In Naomi Klein's words,[6]

Fundamentally, the task is to articulate not just an alternative set of policy proposals but an alternative worldview to rival the one at the heart of the ecological crisis—embedded in interdependence rather than hyper-individualism, reciprocity rather than dominance, and cooperation rather than hierarchy.

In thinking about how to meet this need—about what a new moral vision should accomplish—I came to two clear conclusions. First, to integrate the imperative of ecological understanding with interconnected justice issues, we must replace the "twin towers" of the neoliberal worldview: the privilege of self-interest and greed at the heart of "Economic Man" and the notions of supremacy and domination built into the "Social Darwinist" view of humanity. Second, to get to the heart of the matter, we must make a clean break with the historical roots of neoliberalism and formulate the new moral system through the lens of 21st-century reality, resting on 21st-century premises.

The phrase "21st century" is shorthand for all the ways that we understand ourselves and our planet differently now than our nation's forefathers did when they cast the original die for our political economy. Our current understandings encompass changes over the last century in our knowledge of evolution and ecology (i.e., the dynamic history of our planet, and of life on earth, and how all of life is interrelated), and insights from the cognitive and social sciences (about human brains, minds, culture, and society). A moral system grounded in today's knowledge makes different assumptions about the nature of reality, history, our planet, and our species than the corresponding prior assumptions built into the theories behind and terminology of neoliberal economic and political discourse. As Walter Lippman's epigraph asserts, these concepts are the core elements of all moral codes.

I typically call natural humanism a "worldview"—another word for an all-encompassing belief system—but it could just as well be called a "conceptual framework" or a social, moral, or political "philosophy." It is an original synthesis of Big Ideas from the cognitive, social, and biological sciences. The heart of the project was to identify the core fundamental premises from which to construct this new contemporary worldview. Premises are the essential distinguishing feature of any belief system or conceptual framework. I aspired to make these premises as self-justifying as possible by grounding them in empirical knowledge and a species-wide universality. I then used them to address enduring moral dilemmas, instinctively believing that the resulting worldview would cohere and make sense as a whole.

Core Premises of Natural Humanism

Natural humanism rests on two foundational premises: naturalism and social constructionism. *Naturalism* is logically prior to social constructionism because its first axiom is that the "natural" world is the only world that exists. The concept of a supernatural or transcendent source of truth, explanation, or virtue is solely a creation of the human imagination. *Humanity is made entirely of nature.* We (including our bodies, cultures, economies, and beliefs) are encompassed by and enmeshed in the natural world, continuously interacting with nature on a hierarchy of levels from metabolism within individuals through our whole species with the whole biosphere. Given this premise, the only possible grounding and source of authority for a moral philosophy is to be found in nature, including a naturalist interpretation of human needs.[7]

Social constructionism is best understood in the context of "the human condition," our unique niche in nature. Humans are at once fully animal and distinctively mindful, the only species living in civilizations of their own creation. By virtue of this unique niche, a wide range of existential dilemmas are common to the subjective experience of all human beings, individually and collectively. Like all animals, our biological propensities are predetermined by evolutionary history. And, like all higher primates, humans are biologically prepared for active social, emotional, and mental lives.

However, our unique, definitive biological heritage is our capacity for open-ended symbolic representation, with which *we collectively construct our own social reality* in the medium of culture. Humans construct social reality (including language, traditions, norms, laws, institutions, and identities) through continuing interactions with their respective local, national, and global cultures. Although some other animals create elements of their own cultures, only humans are literally *constituted* by culture through their interactions with the culture in which they are raised.

At the same time, humanity is an interconnected part of nature, totally dependent on nature's health for our existence and survival. Human freedom can exist only within nature's constraints, which include the laws of physics, the ecological dynamics of life on earth, and our individual and species biological needs and limits. Within these constraints, *human possibilities are open-ended*—unlimited—which is existentially both liberating (hopes and dreams) and frightening (terror and despair). Ultimately, it is up to us to determine how our given biological propensities will be actualized and institutionalized in culture.

These premises together imply a natural "unity in diversity." Through universal, species-wide inheritance all humans share the same biological inclinations, existential dilemmas, and constructed social realities. Still, as diversity is ubiquitous in nature, our species manifests great diversity among cultures, each the product of its own unique history and circumstances. As a result, individuals growing up in each culture interact with its unique blend of constitutive elements and internalize the many components of social reality in culturally-specific flavors. Individual variation within each culture adds yet another level of diversity to humanity.

In light of the intrinsic diversity among and within cultures, an additional core premise of natural humanism is the moral imperative of *pluralism*. From cognitive science we know there are no facts without some frame or theory within which to identify them. All frames, theories, and similar conceptual filters manifest the knower's *perspective*. All knowledge is understood from some perspective; there is no such thing as pure, transcendent, perfectly objective knowledge.

Further, there can be no "best" or universal perspective because ultimate reality is so vast and complex, far beyond comprehension from any one perspective. Thus, *all viewpoints are intrinsically limited and incomplete*. For this reason, the proper grounds for valid (socially agreed-upon) knowledge must be cultural practices that embody or embrace multiple perspectives and, therefore, provide a principled basis for legitimate moral authority. Besides pluralism itself (inclusive diversity), the best examples of such practices are deliberative democracy and the skeptical empiricism of the scientific community.

The worldview of natural humanism emerges as the implications of these core premises are fleshed out over the twelve chapters to follow. These premises imply a distinctly different worldview than that of neoliberalism. In fact, they challenge its very foundations.

Challenges to Neoliberalism's Foundations

One foundation of neoliberalism is a *fixed* view of human nature; in particular, the archetype of a self-interested individual. This "economic man" archetype has survived centuries of unquestioned acceptance among political economists and the public alike in no small part because of the underlying assumption that *self-interest is inevitable and immutable.*

In contrast, natural humanism posits an *open-ended* foundational human condition in which all humans are born incomplete hybrids of inherited emotional (animal) predispositions and unlimited mental capacities. *We inherit tendencies, not necessities, and we do not inherit culture, we create it for ourselves.* Because our human condition allows for an open-ended plurality of cultures, norms, institutions, and beliefs, how humans relate to the natural world and to each other is always open to new possibilities, new inventions, and new results (discussed in chapter one).

In particular, domination hierarchies and "economic man" institutions—the two main pillars of the neoliberal regime—are ripe for replacement by new, constructive, moral, and sustainable ways of living. These alternatives, embodied in natural humanism, are developed in the chapters to follow. The central issues to be explored can be briefly summarized as follows:

As to the first pillar, authorities in support of domination hierarchies (prime examples are "Earth belongs to humans," colonialism, slavery, racism, and patriarchy) use *presumptive supremacy* to legitimate unequal, exploitive power and money regimes (chapters three, eight, and nine). However, as we know today, (a) humanity's fate has always been up to Nature, not vice versa (chapter six); (b) genetically and existentially, humans are all one species; *alleged superiority is a discretionary cultural relation, not a fixed biological one* (chapter eight); and (c) the actual order of life on Earth consists of networks of interdependent ecologies, within which domination hierarchies exist only as means to limited ends in local contexts (chapter five).

So natural humanism rejects as illegitimate all forms of authority claimed or taken in the name of an alleged "natural order" or "higher power." There is simply no such order or power, no such source of legitimate authority. Legitimate authority requires transparent accountability and derives from collective decisions of free and willing followers to grant such power to a leader, position, or principle (chapter three). The ideal expression of legitimate authority is self-government, as manifested in an inclusive and egalitarian participative democracy (chapter ten).

As to the second pillar, the sanctity of private property rights is the linchpin of neoliberal economics. While government power is inherently constrained by law, merchant power is unconstrained by default. *The burden of proof is on the public* to justify constraints on the uses of private property and the pursuit of profits. In particular, private property owners *acting lawfully* do not have to account on their balance sheets for "externalities" such as the environmental and social commons. The most fundamental costs thus ignored, and borne by the public, are (a) the destructive climate effects of burning fossil fuels and (b) the denial of social justice from the domination of political power by private capital.

From the perspective of natural humanism, we cannot survive without healthy physical and social environments (chapters nine and ten); Earth's biosphere and humanity's social fabric belong to everyone, the common "property" of our species. Rather than build a political economy around the archetype of an individual profit-seeking "economic man," natural humanism embeds and interconnects all humans within the environmental and social commons that sustain and nourish them.

Both private property rights and profit-seeking could—and in the U.S. undoubtedly would—remain major elements of the political and economic system. But they may trump the interests of the environmental or social *commons* only if an exception is granted explicitly by an inclusive democratic process on a case-by-case basis. By default, *the burden of proof is on private property owners* to justify "taking" from common resources without prior negotiated restitution and appropriate limitations. Thus, natural humanism "flips the script" of neoliberalism at its core.

The issues described here arise organically at many points in the chapters ahead. The combined effect of the foundational differences between the worldviews of neoliberalism and natural humanism is a profound divergence between them, which is summarized by Table 1 in the book's concluding chapter. However, the primary purpose of this book is not to critique neoliberalism per se, but rather to develop and justify a manifestly better, alternative way of life. Natural humanism has its own logic and moral foundation that must stand on its own feet. The structure of this book is crafted to present the best case for this worldview, from its premises and moral principles through their full implications.

A Roadmap of the Book

Which Future? is sequenced in three parts that build cumulatively to convey the full picture of natural humanism. The first two parts provide foundational knowledge of society and nature necessary to understand the moral system that integrates them. Part III presents and elaborates the moral code itself, and then imagines how a natural humanistic society might function.

The book begins with chapters on *Culture*, *Sense Making*, and what it means to say that we effectively live in our *Belief Systems*. Part I as a whole explains the social construction of reality and introduces many topics that will be brought up again later, including existential dilemmas, paradigms, and a central issue of natural humanism, identifying the sources of legitimate authority. The key takeaway from Part I is that because human reality is socially constructed, we are not so much inheritors of a given world as *creators* of it. We can replace today's dominant but dysfunctional neoliberal worldview by changing the way we think about ourselves and the world. Social constructionism is a truly empowering perspective.[8] Embracing our role as co-constructors of our own belief systems energizes us to take on challenges ahead.

Part II contains four chapters about how nature works, how humanity fits into nature, and how humanity's survival depends on keeping the biosphere healthy. The opening *Systems Thinking* chapter reviews the basic concepts of how systems work through feedback processes and hierarchical levels. *Living Systems* then surveys the biology of life on Earth, providing enough substance to prepare the reader for the linchpin chapter, *Humanity's Relationship To Nature*, where the book turns a corner from mainly descriptive material to a series of chapters concerned with normative issues. I argue here that we should look to nature for moral guidance. Part II ends with *Life's Healthy Operating Principles*, which summarizes the systems dynamics and operating principles that account for the biosphere's continuing good health. Understanding nature's dynamics (and how we fit into them) to this degree is needed to appreciate the aspiration of natural humanism to meet this moment in history with a moral system appropriate to the magnitude of the climate crisis.

Having now covered the needed foundational knowledge of society and nature, Part III presents the worldview of natural humanism in five chapters focused successively on general approach, living sustainably, justice from a humanist perspective, new possibilities, and a summary with implications. *Naturalist Morality* asks what morality amounts to when we rely solely on what we can learn from the study of nature and human experience, and provides illustrative answers in brief discussions of three existential dilemmas: Us versus Them, Domination versus Partnership, and Self-Interest versus Community Concern.

Life's Lessons for Sustainability derives normative values, goals, and strategies for humanity from the patterns and principles identified earlier in the Part II chapter, *Life's Healthy Operating Principles.* The ten lessons encompass how humanity should relate to planet Earth; how people should relate to each other; how to use feedback control systems to achieve sustainability in human affairs; and a proposal for a built-in "immune system" for society emphasizing participatory democracy, science, and diversity/pluralism as first principles.

The *Humanist Values and Principles* chapter considers how to promote and celebrate the health, well-being, and fulfillment of all human beings equally. I contend that basic needs, instinctive curiosity, and the triad of autonomy, self-determination, and agency are keys to unlocking human potential, and demand moral attention, because of the harm suffered from their neglect and the great benefits reaped from their proper support. The chapter delineates the social and political conditions needed for this support, including everyone's equal right not to be coerced by physical force, poverty, or hidden psychological manipulation.

In these first three chapters of Part III, solutions to core social justice issues are construed as inevitable consequences of the transformative changes necessary to achieve the health, well-being, and fulfillment of all human beings equally.

In the following chapter, *Toward A Natural Humanist Society*, I look ahead, inviting readers to suspend disbelief for the sake of imagining new possibilities. What changes might we expect to see in society if there were to be a meaningful shift in belief from the established neoliberal worldview toward natural humanism? I then propose several transformative strategies and policies, not as presumptive solutions but as exemplary goals and suggestions for experimentation. For example, to replace the economic growth imperative of free-market capitalism with continuous improvement toward sustainability, we must not only change what is measured (new goals) but also create a regulatory framework (new system) within which cycles of feedback drive continually-evolving targeted policies (new method).

The concluding chapter, *Summary and Implications*, sums up the book in two ways: first, with a table highlighting key elements of divergence between the neoliberal and natural humanist worldviews, and second, by spelling out the three main tenets of natural humanism and their key implications.

———

One cannot read (or write) a book about moral choices or prospects without wondering how plausible the ideas are. I have my own doubts about the likelihood of a shift in worldview at significant scale within a decade; anyone reading chapters two and three of this book will find plenty of support for a skeptical stance. But my doubts about a "happy ending" for natural humanism are dwarfed by my fear of a continuing neoliberal regime, which has already done so much damage to our environmental and social commons and offers no hope of fending off ultimate disasters.

In any case, it should be clear that *Which Future?* does not in any way try to address issues of plausibility. Rather, the book aims to present *a holistic vision of what could and should be*—a coherent, timely, and constructive alternative to a stagnant status quo. I made a conscious, affirmative decision not to allow potential implementation roadblocks to deter me from setting forth what I believe to be the most desirable outcomes.

Which Future? encompasses both biological and cultural dynamics while maintaining a fundamental distinction between them.[9] All meaningful biological factors are species-wide; they are universal among humans. Cultural factors, by contrast, incorporate the unique history of each culture, so the same universal dilemmas are resolved differently from one culture to another. It follows that each culture's interpretation of natural humanism will have its own distinctive slant. With this diversity in mind, I aim throughout the book to develop *general* principles that can, and must, be adapted to culturally-specific circumstances.

To give those principles added concreteness and focus, I write from my perspective as an American, knowing only too well how atypical we often are when compared with other countries and cultures, and how insistent some of us can be that our way is the only way. Given the existential dilemmas common to all cultures, however, I hope and expect that my examples from American society will find meaningful counterparts in other countries, while deferring judgment to readers of their precise relevance and applicability.

I also want to foretell a consequence of writing a high-level synthesis of many important ideas from multiple disciplines. As a description of a coherent, all-encompassing belief system at a higher level, *Which Future?* inevitably omits specific details and nuances of the important ideas it incorporates. Readers left wanting more detail and nuance about these component ideas are urged to consult the Notes and Further Reading sections in the back of the book.

Finally, my aim is to offer natural humanism as a hopeful, forward-looking, and above all, *timely* moral philosophy—a worldview that can help guide us toward the intertwined goals of sustainability and social justice. As such, *Which Future?* aspires to play a role in the process of institutional change by reframing issues to overcome existing mental models and core beliefs, and by introducing alternative perspectives—ideas that can change our understanding of the world.[10] My hope is that readers in the worlds of activism, policymaking, and communications will find this vision a timely and useful framework to inspire and guide concrete courses of action.

PART I

HUMAN REALITY IS SOCIALLY CONSTRUCTED

Man is biologically predestined to construct and inhabit a world with others. This world becomes for him the dominant and definitive reality.

— Peter Berger & Thomas Luckmann (1966)[1]

The first part of the book explains the social construction of reality. This subject comes first as it is foundational to the whole argument for natural humanism. It is only—and precisely—because humans construct social reality ourselves that we are able, if willing, to replace an established but dysfunctional worldview with a better one.

To think this way about social reality is unconventional and nonintuitive. In common experience, reality is what we all find to be given, inherited, or received "out there," as it has always been. The alternative perspective I present here is a synthesis of what anthropologists, sociologists, psychologists, and evolutionary biologists have learned about the role of *culture* in human experience over the past seven decades or so. The three chapters of Part I spell out the key concepts and implications of this contemporary point of view.

1
CULTURE

There is no such thing as a human nature independent of culture. ... We are, in sum, incomplete or unfinished animals who complete or finish ourselves through culture.

— **Clifford Geertz (1973)**[1]

The Human Condition

"The human condition" refers to the subjectivity of human experience, an existential state of being, the inescapable fate of being born *Homo sapiens*. The concept of the human *condition* is entirely different from the traditional idea of human *nature*, that certain characteristics or dispositions are fixed and inevitable because (God or) evolution made us that way. To say a trait is human nature is to claim that it is inherited and predetermined. Take, for example, the key premise of neoliberal economic theory, that self-interest is pivotal to human nature, a dominant motivation of the entire species.

Claims like that about human nature are commonly used to explain and justify self-serving behavior. In this vein, selfish behaviors are not only *caused* by biological inheritance but also are the *causes* of many other behaviors. For example, "it's just human nature to be self-interested; that's why she voted against public housing in her neighborhood." This kind of reasoning epitomizes the social determinism which natural humanism rejects.

By contrast, the human condition is not a set of pre-determined traits. It doesn't cause anything; it is the open-ended existential state that manifests our essential uniqueness in being both fully animal and distinctively mindful. Importantly, it is the source of a wide range of existential dilemmas common to the subjective experience of all human beings by virtue of our unique niche in nature—the only animal species living in a civilization of its own creation.

Like all animals, we do have biological propensities predetermined by evolutionary history. And, like all higher primates, humans are biologically prepared for active social, emotional, and mental lives. However, our unique, definitive biological heritage is the brain's capacity for open-ended symbolic representation, with which we collectively construct our own reality in the medium of culture.[2] Humans are literally *constituted* by culture.

At the same time, humanity is an interconnected part of nature, totally dependent on nature's health for our existence and survival. Human freedom can exist only within nature's constraints, which include laws of physics, ecological dynamics of life on earth, and our individual and species biological needs and limits. Within these constraints, human possibilities are open-ended—unlimited—which is existentially both liberating (hopes and dreams) and frightening (terror and despair). Ultimately, it is up to us to determine how our given biological propensities will be actualized and institutionalized in culture.

Constituting Ourselves In and Through Culture

People have never stopped wondering, "How are humans different from other animals?" Years ago, when human fossils were found alongside stone age remnants of early tools, tool use was thought to be the key difference—until we learned more about widespread tool use among animals. The next viable candidate for principal difference-maker was language. But the more deeply the concept of language is broken down, and the more closely animals are studied in their own habitats, the more nuanced and complex this distinction becomes. From sky to sea, animals use sounds constantly to signal to each other. The more complex their social lives, the more nuanced their use of language-like vocalization. Since even syntax is a matter of degree (there are elements of syntax in some animal vocalizations), its role as the ultimate criterion of fully -human language is increasingly contested.

The indisputably unique characteristic of fully-human language, however, is its unlimited capacity to stand for or express any kind of thought or idea. As Terrence Deacon explains in *The Symbolic Species,* this infinite flexibility is the result of a *precursor* to language, the brain's ability to reference the world symbolically, thereby to construct networks of meaning. Deacon argues convincingly that the open-ended, extensible way our brains use symbols is one definitive differentiator between humans and other higher primates.[3] Other animals communicate with each other very effectively with sounds and gestures that signify important feelings, actions, and events, but they do not employ extensible symbols the way that humans do.

In this context *extensibility* means that symbols can refer to anything, including other symbols. This is the fundamental property that enables the construction of networks of meaning in which words refer to other words, as in a dictionary; words refer to ideas; and ideas refer to other ideas, as in the extension from the concept of money to the concept of credit to the concept of market economies. Crucially, extensibility also enables *self*-consciousness, and reflection on our own thinking, the loops and levels of human-created complex systems, including most algorithms, and the unlimited creative possibilities found in all forms of artistic expression. It allows imagination to run wild, creating fictional characters and fictional worlds,[4] including the comprehensive belief systems that humans effectively live in (explored in chapter three). It is not an exaggeration to posit that *Homo sapiens'* unlimited, extensible symbol use became the platform for cultural evolution, a fundamentally different, emergent level of natural evolution.

Among higher social animals with complex emotional lives (bonobos and chimpanzees), mental capacities including consciousness, empathy and cooperation are highly developed; also present are rudimentary forms of imagination, self-reference, and planning (in problem-solving contexts). Studies of other notable social animals like dolphins and elephants reveal further evidence of higher cognitive faculties and rich emotional lives. In fact, it's difficult these days to identify any basic cognitive or emotional process allegedly unique to humans that can't be found somewhere in the nonhuman animal world—except our open-ended, extensible symbol use.

In addition, from a different perspective, there is a broad consensus that human civilization in all its incarnations manifests a *scale of intentional cooperation* vastly exceeding anything seen elsewhere in nature.[5] Probing deeply into our unique mental capacities related to cooperation, recent experimental research captures the step-by-step development of *shared intentionality* in young children, using related behaviors in higher apes as points of comparison. Drawing on this research base in *Becoming Human*, Michael Tomasello presents a compelling theory linking a uniquely human cluster of motivational and cognitive skills to successive stages of children's progression into culture.[6] In other research, Jerome Bruner's case studies reveal a similar step-by-step pattern in how children pick up their native culture's "folk psychology" implicitly while *learning to tell stories*, because the culture's norms, values, and rules are built into the ordinary, intention-laden use of language that children absorb from practice.[7] Both sets of research findings emphasize the child's active role in seeking out and soaking up the specific meanings their culture provides.

This child-driven, enculturation version of human uniqueness, with its focus on our exceptional capacity for intentional cooperative behavior, is perfectly compatible with the version based on our brain's open-ended, extensible use of symbols. Deacon identifies a specific brain capacity allowing humans to develop complex networks of meaning, individually and collectively. The enculturation research documents how humans begin life with a program for absorbing the networks of meaning in the specific culture they inhabit. These two distinct levels of description and explanation in tandem provide a deeper understanding of human uniqueness than either does by itself.

The gradual evolution of networks of meaning in language, together with collective intentional cooperation, would have enabled early humans to communicate and coordinate functions while maintaining cohesion effectively in larger and larger groups. This seems a plausible candidate for the "origin story" of culture. It is obviously of great intrinsic interest to tell our origin story as accurately and meaningfully as we can. It will be fascinating to watch the further development of research and theorizing on this subject.

———————

Like humans, many other animals are born "unfinished," in the basic physical sense that they are unable to survive without parental care until their brains and bodies reach some level of independent function. During this protected childhood they learn how to navigate and survive in their ecological niche. Social animals teach social skills to their young, largely by imitation. But *unlike* humans, what remains to be finished after birth is prescribed by and limited to the inherited blueprint of the species. *All non-human animals live in the natural world as they find it.*

Humans are not only born unfinished; we are born incomplete. Uniquely and definitively, the blueprint of *Homo sapiens* is to constitute ourselves within the specific culture into which we are born.[8] By inheritance, as human infants reach developmental milestones, they *proactively* engage adults in reciprocal communications, eliciting from caregivers just what they need to learn to move on to the next level. Each new developmental level expands the child's social and language skill set, naturally incorporating the speech patterns, habits, and norms of the culture.

Humans co-evolve with culture. As a culture evolves, growing up in that culture becomes a new experience as each successive generation produces individuals with different skills and concerns from the preceding one. And as humans evolve, collectively, so do their cultures, adapting and adopting new technologies, media, and value systems into its continuing institutions. The relationship between individuals and their cultural milieu is bi-directional, a co-construction process.[9] The individual side of this process is intuitive: how we "create ourselves" out of the building blocks of the cultural milieu, how we forge our identities by latching on to certain roles and images while rejecting others. It is intuitive because we all subjectively experience ourselves going through this unavoidable process.

However, the other side of this mutual construction process—the dynamic by which the "systems that were already in place"[10] had been created by the people who preceded us—is not intuitive at all. On the contrary, we instinctively assume the cultural world in which we find ourselves is the one and only, given, objective reality. This is a universal illusion. Each culture sees reality its own way, through its unique lens, having always known it to be that way. Thus, all of us naturally *reify* our culture, meaning that we don't apprehend our own interactive, dynamic role in creating it; instead, we simply live in it. More precisely, we subjectively live in our *beliefs* about this world, as both sides of the co-construction dynamic continue, day in and day out, throughout our lifetimes. In this sense *we are like fish in water, except that we co-construct the very "water" we live in.*

Human incompleteness is the essence of our difference from all other organisms. It is at once a gift and a burden. We must be inventors of our own social reality, and are free to do it however we can. We are required by our biological inheritance to complete ourselves through culture and, at the level of culture, we are unlimited in how we can accomplish this. We are limited only by nature's constraints, which include the laws of physics, ecological dynamics of life on earth, and our individual and species biological needs and limits. Thus, the need to make sense of our experience—to embrace a system of thought within which our lives can have meaning—is as inseparable from the human condition as the need to breathe and feed ourselves.

Existential Dilemmas and Cultural Pluralism

Existential dilemmas are a fundamental part of the human condition because (a) we biologically inherit the necessity of constructing reality ourselves, through culture, and, (b) within nature's constraints, we are *unlimited* in how we accomplish this. Most of these dilemmas are intrinsically cultural and negotiated distinctively on the basis of the particular history and nature of social relationships in each culture. These include dilemmas about how to make sense of the physical world as well as how to make sense of the social world.

Beyond the fundamental dimensions of space and time, the physical world is amenable to description in terms of parts and wholes, substances (things) and forms (patterns), networks and hierarchies, and structures and processes. For all these dichotomies (and others), it's safe to say that there is no useful way to understand the world without taking both sides of the dichotomy into account. (Reality *does* consist of *both* parts and wholes.) Yet they qualify as existential dilemmas because different cultures routinely favor one side over the other. In particular, the many cultures comprising Western civilization generally emphasize parts over wholes, substances over forms, hierarchies over networks, and structures over processes. This way of perceiving reality corresponds to the analytic/mechanistic viewpoint of traditional Western science. In contrast, East Asian cultures generally perceive reality more in terms of holistic patterns and interconnected, interdependent relationships. These different perspectives toward the physical world closely parallel long histories of different social relationships in their respective cultures.[11]

In the social world, the most complex and impactful dilemma is "us" versus "them." Like all social animals, humans inherit a predisposition to act prosocially (trusting, cooperatively) toward our own clan, and with suspicion if not hostility toward outsiders. Who is inside and who is outside may be based on familiarity (status or class), appearance (skin color), territory (nationality), beliefs (religious or political ideology), or something totally arbitrary. However, emotions and behavioral expression of these tendencies are profoundly affected by how family, teachers, political leaders, and other cultural influences define *otherness*. At the extremes, the inner circle may be drawn very tightly (literally, one's own clan) or extended to all of humanity (as by some spiritual leaders). Each culture's enduring practices concerning us versus them derive predominantly from its unique history, circumstances, and pattern of social relationships (aka "social structure").[12]

Another major social dilemma is domination versus cooperation. Again, humans inherit a tendency to jockey for status and rank among individuals. But they also inherit a predisposition to cooperate (and generally behave prosocially) among the group, tribe, or clan in which they are raised. Each culture's management of these two tendencies can take many forms, again, depending on its history and circumstances. Another closely related social dilemma is self-interest versus community concern. These dimensions overlap with each other, so we would expect them to cluster together in patterns of varying strength from culture to culture. We will take a close look at this particular set of existential social dilemmas later, in chapter eight, "Naturalist Morality."

At the hub of many intersecting cultural dimensions is the distinction between an *in*dependent self and an *inter*dependent self. Predictably, this contrast mirrors the analytic versus holistic split between Western and East Asian cultures. An independent self is an individual first and a member of society second. This priority imbues child-rearing in most Western cultures, including parenting, schooling, and the basic structure of social relations. In contrast, an interdependent self learns to think of herself primarily in terms of how others will feel and react to her actions, and only secondarily about her own feelings. This ethos of interconnected and interdependent social relationships pervades society in most East Asian cultures.[13]

From the standpoint of morality, the central aspect of a culture is, what makes a good person? The answer hews closely to the definition of an ideal self, which in turn relates to the culture's ideal positions along the dimensions of cooperation and community concern. Thus, a good person in most Western cultures exhibits individualist virtues like self-esteem and personal success, while in most East Asian cultures she manifests relational values, like empathy, cooperation, and community concern. These emphases are relative, of course, and tempered by a sense of balance in all but the most extreme subcultures. In addition, virtually all cultures adhere to generally prosocial moral principles such as "do unto others" and "do no harm."

If each culture evolves its distinctive ideals and social structure from the unique history and circumstances of its inhabitants, and if morality is grounded in those distinctive cultural ideals, then good and bad (and right and wrong) can only be defined within the scope and context of each particular culture (or belief system, or worldview). *Morality is intrinsically bound to its own distinctive cultural context.* It does not make sense to judge the behavior of a person from culture A by the standards of culture B, or vice versa, because each individual has been raised and socialized ("enculturated") into the norms and values of their own culture. But that does not mean that every aspect of every culture needs to be regarded as morally equal! I will address concerns about "moral relativism" in chapter three, "Belief Systems."

One can choose to focus on similarities across cultures as well as differences. The similarities derive from our species-wide human condition: the biological predispositions and existential dilemmas that individuals in all cultures share. When social scientists look for similarities, they can derive measurable dimensions along which all national cultures vary by applying statistical techniques (such as factor analysis) to huge databases of survey data. One exemplary framework, developed by Geert Hofstede, describes national cultures along six major dimensions: Power Distance (how inequality is understood), Individualism and Collectivism, Uncertainty Avoidance, Gender Differences, Short-term and Long-term Orientation, and Indulgence versus Restraint.[14] Hofstede points out that national cultures and organizational cultures differ so much from each other that they cannot even be measured on the same dimensions. The results of such international comparisons are overwhelming evidence of the diversity and variety of national (and organizational) cultures. In addition, of course, individuals vary greatly among themselves within any culture.

This diversity—the inherent multiplicity—of norms, values, and viewpoints across cultures compels us to accept, honor, and embrace a *pluralist* approach to all species-wide issues of morality and legitimate authority. All singular viewpoints (including natural humanism) are limited and incomplete. Multiple perspectives are *always* necessary for decisions to be granted legitimate authority, and always beneficial to establishing the validity and reliability of empirical findings. Diversity among individuals within a culture is as prevalent as it is among cultures (notwithstanding attempts by authoritarians to squelch it). Thus, the pluralist imperative for our whole species also applies perforce to any group of humans large enough to encompass multiple perspectives; certainly to all cultures and nations, and perhaps, these days, to any organization or state with a commitment to justice. Issues of diversity and pluralism will be revisited in chapter three and in Part III of this book.

The overall takeaway from this chapter is that culture is the medium, the soup, and the environment in which all the "sense making" of humans is created, expressed, contested, institutionalized, and acted out. Each culture co-evolves with its members, providing individuals inside the culture with the raw materials of self and identity, and affecting other cultures worldwide through movies, shows, and social media, and, via the global economy, planet Earth.

The rest of Part I explores the ways and means by which humans and cultures construct each other. Chapter two focuses on how we make sense of the world at the individual and group levels, from intuition and rationality to socially shared models of how we think and work together. Chapter three shifts focus to the societal level to examine the ins and outs of belief systems, worldviews, and the crucial difference between absolute and legitimate authority.

2
SENSE MAKING

As we saw in chapter one, young children begin to make sense of their culture's norms, values, and rules by practicing its spoken language and learning to construct meaningful sentences out of the basic units of objects, actions, and relationships. These elementary linguistic structures are the building blocks of stories, models, and concepts, the familiar, higher-level structures which humans use to make sense of the world and themselves. Stories, models, and concepts, in turn, are the building blocks of belief systems and worldviews, the most complex and comprehensive mental structures (to be discussed in chapter three).

Meaning Derives from Context

By themselves, however, these mental structures are like the frame of a house or the skeleton of a body without the distinctive fleshing out that personalizes them. The missing ingredient is the *meaning* of the actions, events, and facts that claim our attention in the flow of experience, from everyday conversations to epic questions like "Why are we here?"

Meaning derives from context. Different types of actions, events, or facts require different types of contexts to supply their meaning; but in all cases the entity's meaning is given by the context. What is the intention, purpose, or goal of an action? What is the sense, import, or significance of an event or story? What is the explanation or interpretation of a fact? The meaning of balls and strikes derives from the rules of baseball. The meaning of a sunset depends on whether the context is astronomy or romance.

Understanding the context answers the (typically implicit) question "what does this thing mean?" because context is the very source of meaning. So changing the context of something necessarily changes its meaning. The same interpersonal touching that is normative in a consensual context is disreputable in a nonconsensual context. It is obviously of great importance to get the context right in this case, but this principle holds more generally.

Getting the context right is a major preoccupation of the intuitive system of the brain, which works relentlessly in the background—outside consciousness—to figure out which situations and feelings are relevant to the present moment; in other words, to decide *the most appropriate context* within which to make sense of current actions and events. In daily life we rarely pause to think consciously about what things mean. The brain not only identifies proper contexts for us in the background but also interprets the meaning of actions, events, and facts in terms of those contexts. Thus, we normally make sense of our experience in real time as if on automatic pilot.[1]

Contexts are pliable configurations of elements that collectively define an overall setting, as well as details and nuances of particular scenes, situations, or circumstances. Hence each element in a given context may potentially be decisive in distinguishing one meaning from another. For example, consider a conversation in which the phrase "if you insist" is spoken. Here the phrase's meaning is strongly implied by the tone or vibe of the conversation: playful, if a friendly vibe; polite, if a neutral vibe; and sarcastic, if a hostile vibe. The importance of vibe as a factor is the same whether the conversation occurs in a scene from a movie, a negotiation between nations, or in your own life. The distinguishing clue could come from the conversationalists' histories, the setting behind them, their physical postures, or their tone of voice.

The presence or absence of just one element in a context may be decisive in determining the meaning of an event or outcome. Consider the importance of each item of evidence in decisions about whether to hire someone, or the innocence or guilt of a defendant on trial. Decision makers are particularly attuned to getting "the complete picture," knowing that critical inferences and attributions are suspect if a key element is missing from the ledger. The entire outcome (and legitimacy) of a trial can rest on what evidence is admitted or excluded. The same logic applies to any "blind spot" obscuring vital information about our own thinking processes. We do not make consequential decisions on the basis of incomplete information if we can help it.

Yet incomplete knowledge about how our own brains work is both normal and inevitable, and it has significant implications for how we see ourselves in relation to reality. No one sees the complete picture of reality itself. We see only our own version of it, created by our own brain, which makes sense of ongoing experience on the basis of such factors as our unique history, personality, preferences, and prejudices—even our immediate thoughts. Nevertheless, all of us assume by default that what we see is what everyone sees—something like an "objective" reality.[2] This is a universal illusion because none of us is privy to anyone else's projections, nor are we aware that our own subjective experience of reality is a projection of our brain (unless we think about it while reading a paragraph like this one).

I consider this phenomenon to be a persistent "blind spot" obscuring vital information because it is responsible for two consequential misattributions concerning the construction of social reality. The first one was discussed in chapter one: the fact that we do not recognize our own role as creators of culture. Because we are not aware of our own role, we attribute social reality to other factors, even if we cannot specify them; this misattribution is called "reifying" our culture.

The second misattribution concerns subjectivity. Because each person sees only their own, unique version of reality, no one can truly claim to speak for anyone else. This understanding of *the inevitability of subjectivity* undergirds the premises of diversity and pluralism in this book. It does not mean that anything goes; it means that multiple viewpoints must be included in principle because each one has inherent limitations. Only by combining multiple viewpoints can we see the whole picture, as illuminated in the ancient parable of the six blind men each touching and describing a different part of an elephant.

If we grasp what it means for each brain to project its own unique version of reality—and that that projection is actually what we see when we perceive the external world—then two very broad and deep ideas follow: (1) the capacity for agency and causality in each human brain, enabling it to "bring forth" each person's contribution to the culture at large; and (2) the unavoidable, intrinsic subjectivity of all perceptions and interpretations, and therefore of any assertions based on them. The first insight exposes the illusion called "reifying," i.e., that culture is given to us rather than created. The second insight exposes the "objectivity illusion," i.e., that the world we see is an objective one that everyone else sees, too, rather than a personal, subjective one based on each person's unique experiences.

Let me restate these conclusions in terms of context. We cannot fathom our own role in the construction of social reality while our context for understanding it is missing the crucial fact that our experience of the world "out there" is a projection of our unique brain. Without some special effort to take this piece of evidence into account, everyone assumes they see what everyone else sees. When the explanatory context expands to include this piece of evidence, we can recognize an agency and causal mechanism in our brain that was invisible before. The meaning we take from the whole context now includes our capacity as individuals to be co-creators of our social reality. It also necessarily includes an appreciation of the inherent subjectivity of all perception. As we shall see, these deeper meanings and understandings have great potential to enhance human capacities for constructive social interaction.

Intuition and Rationality

Thinking and feeling *always* interact in our minds and overt behavior, yet it is sometimes useful to discuss one or the other independently. In the previous section, without taking emotions into account, we saw how attributions are sensitive to specific elements of a context, particularly missing pieces of evidence. In this section, we begin to explore how emotions and feelings influence sense making.

The human brain includes two distinct systems for thinking, both of which operate continuously; I refer to them here as "intuition" and "rationality."[3] Intuition originates in the older part of the brain and is well-attuned to our emotions, needs, and desires. It knows only what is happening in the moment, and uses familiarity, association, and coherence as sufficient criteria to jump rapidly to conclusions. By contrast, rationality requires conscious effort, works slowly, and serves the interests of the person we think we are, or would like to be. It can incorporate past and hypothetical experience, principles, rules, and other abstract concepts, bringing them all to bear on the present moment. Thus, rationality is required for reflection, willpower, self-control, and making comparisons and important decisions, as well as for keeping intuition in check.

Although rationality wants to think it runs the show, most of the brain's heavy lifting is done by intuition and other memory-intensive processes working automatically, outside consciousness.[4] As we interact with the environment, the brain continuously updates its detailed working models of internal and external reality. Concurrently, everything committed to long term memory through attention, thought, experience, and expertise acquired, say, via artistic or athletic training or academic studies, gets integrated within these working models, including all associated feelings.

Expert performance of any kind requires training memory purposefully until intuition can take over, at which point conscious attention is free to concentrate on expression and strategic adaptation to emerging circumstances (as well as further learning). Such extensive training, together with a lifetime of offloading knowledge and experience from rationality to intuition, helps to demystify how so much of our mental and emotional life can occur under the hood, outside consciousness.

One of rationality's main jobs is to monitor and control thoughts and actions put forward by intuition, allowing some to be expressed directly in behavior while suppressing or modifying others. But attention and energy are limited resources, so when we are otherwise busy, distracted, or just plain lazy, rationality often accepts by default whatever intuition proposes. This dynamic underlies most of the numerous biases and illusions (departures from rationality) that cognitive science research has identified over the past five decades.[5] The best-known of these, "confirmation bias," is the universal propensity to seek out facts that support what we already believe, and to ignore or deny facts that challenge our beliefs.

Rationality can also be compromised by (tacit and unconscious) desires to relieve mental stress, whether from conflicting thoughts, negative judgments, or social pressure. One familiar example is "cognitive dissonance," the tendency to adjust one's attitudes to relieve mental discomfort from holding two conflicting thoughts at once.[6] Another example is the universal inclination to rationalize unworthy behavior after the fact to relieve the discomfort of feeling bad about oneself.[7] A third familiar example is "groupthink," the disposition of individuals in policy-making and problem-solving groups to shift from multiple points of view to a common way of thinking to avoid the stress of social disharmony.[8]

It has been understood for millennia that emotions like fear, sexual arousal, and hatred subvert rationality by hijacking the brain's capacities to attend to anything else. It is also common knowledge that being exhausted or emotionally upset makes it nearly impossible to do difficult mental work. This connection is due to the fact that mental work actually draws from the same (limited) energy source as emotional and physical work; specifically, that the effort expended to sustain willpower, self-control, or any difficult mental work causes one's blood glucose level to drop significantly.[9] Depleting too much energy from the shared pool often requires a recharge before any further work can be done.

At this point, it should be clear that rationality operates efficiently and effectively only under certain conditions, which may be far removed from the emotional demands and cognitive overload of ordinary life. From hungry students in classrooms to exhausted hospital interns or other workers on graveyard shifts, we often require attention and energy from people who are not physiologically capable of delivering it, so they predictably fail to meet expectations. It would make more sense to limit expectations for rationality and expert performance to circumstances carved out and maintained to provide the necessary conditions for it.

Although I have emphasized differences between intuition and rationality so far, in practice, the two systems complement and generally work well with each other. In the dynamic between them, intuition requires training and direction from rationality to integrate personal experience and cultural contexts into its vast network of associative memory, to ensure that intuition's hasty conclusions are based on the best possible working models. Rationality, in turn, requires intuition to integrate its knowledge and experience accurately, so that rationality can count on intuition to handle all thinking effectively that does *not* rely on rationality's exclusive capabilities. In addition, given the constraints on rationality we have noted, it is particularly important for intuition to be able to interrupt and signal rationality proactively when intuition recognizes a situation it cannot handle without assistance.

Emotions, needs, and desires are deeply embedded in this dynamic between intuition and rationality. Intuition has direct access to the brain centers that control our primal emotions, as well as the associative memory network where our feelings are integrated with all other memories. So *everything intuition passes on to rationality is necessarily imbued with emotion*. In turn, intuition's training and direction from rationality incorporates evolving interpretations of its needs and desires as they develop over a lifetime, thereby continually "teaching" intuition how best to fulfill them.

For some people, experiences later in life change their youthful feelings about emotional issues such as race or domination. If those experiences are direct and visceral, they may "reprogram" intuition to manifest the acquired feelings; if not, rationality can always suppress or modify their intuitive expression. People whose rationality is underdeveloped are inevitably at the mercy of their intuition in navigating daily life, especially the strategic emotional messages that permeate today's social, commercial, and media environments. These people are the prime targets of dumbed-down advertising and political propaganda.

Rationality is a vital personal and social capability. Humans cannot get along with each other without reflection, willpower, and self-control, not to speak of the essential role of rationality in cooperation and in all group and social activities. Yet, as we have seen in this brief overview of intuition, rationality, and emotion, sense making always involves interactions among all three systems.[10] One key takeaway is that *virtually all thinking has roots in desires or feelings*, much of it intuitive and outside conscious awareness. Subsequent sections and chapters will build on this insight.

Identity, Emotion, and Beliefs

A central activity of human sense making is the construction of personal identity, an ongoing process of binding oneself emotionally to certain cultural elements but not others. The same kind of selective binding (called "attachment") occurs regularly among animals, the iconic example being newborn ducklings trailing closely behind their mother. Similarly, human parents and their infant children are said to "bond" with each other. Biological attachment emanates from subject to object instinctively, under genetic and hormonal control. The step-by-step symbolic construction of individual identity, however, while otherwise like biological attachment, is an intentional act, an expression of personal preference if not something stronger.[11] Whether intuitive or rational—whether recognized for what it is in the moment or not—each instance of cultural identification reveals a meaningful emotional connection. After all, to a greater or lesser degree, it amounts to a declaration of "This is who I am."

Beliefs are among the most consequential manifestations of identity. *What distinguishes beliefs from mere knowledge is their emotional investment in particular facts, ideas, or people.* Belief in facts or statements means faith and confidence that the facts or statements are true. Belief in ideas means faith and confidence in the "rightness" of what they propose. Belief in people entails faith and confidence that they are "good," so what they say must be true. In the social construction of reality, however, what matters most about beliefs is not so much their verifiability as what those beliefs "say" about the person who believes them. Culturally speaking, beliefs declare identity.

Beliefs are so consequential because cultural identity is emotionally integrated with oneself. *Beliefs shape the mind of the believer*; they are arbiters of trust, faith, and confidence in the very sources of credibility and truth. Once a belief is incorporated into the self, it takes on a life of its own. People become attached to their beliefs and motivated to hold onto them. As noted earlier, *everyone* tends to seek out facts that support what they already believe, and to ignore or deny facts that challenge their beliefs. Moreover, many, perhaps most, beliefs in practices, traditions, or ideologies entail *commitment*, the belief that a certain mode of life merits or deserves support, even though we may find it difficult to live up to it.[12] Commitments serve to justify both some of the most transcendent and the most horrific human behaviors.

Everything said so far about identity, emotion, and belief is as true of groups and larger collections of people as it is of individuals. The corrosive political divisions in the United States at this time are clear illustrations of the power and consequentiality of divergent beliefs as to which set of "facts" to accept as true, and which leaders and media sources to trust. Beliefs connect us emotionally to the social, economic, and political dimensions of the world we live in by carving out the subset of that world we elect to embrace. Thus, in a highly contested political environment, much rides on our stance toward those who carve out a different subset than we do. All too few of us seem to recognize the fundamental subjectivity of our beliefs; increasingly, people seem to act as if their beliefs mirror the world itself. We will pick up this thread more than once in chapter three.

Paradigms

Much individual behavior occurs in socially organized groups and communities that exist for particular social, economic, or political reasons. The term "communities of practice" applies to the full range of such groups and communities, from sports teams and dance companies to corporations, political parties, and religious organizations. As varied in size and purpose as these communities are, they all manifest a similar pattern of social dynamics that accounts for their organization, maintenance, and cohesion under normal circumstances. The name for this ubiquitous pattern is a *paradigm*.[13]

A paradigm encompasses all the ways that members of a particular community of practice make sense of what they do collectively, and how that community organizes and polices itself.[14] For example, all mainstream journalists write within the boundaries of status quo politics, a key element of their paradigm. Thus, a writer knows she risks marginalization by that community if she attacks status quo premises *too* directly. Members of the community all buy into, and are bound together by, their distinctive paradigm, which includes concepts, values, and practices that add up to a shared vision of reality and a model of how to think—and how *not* to think—about the purpose or practices of the community.

A central aspect of any paradigm is the perspective, vision, or *view of reality* shared by that community.[15] A classic example is the world community's historical view of Earth's place in the universe. Until the 17th century, everyone believed the earth to be the center of the universe. After Copernicus proposed the alternative theory that the earth revolves around the sun, and after Galileo used the newly invented telescope to provide observational evidence supporting Copernicus, people gradually began to believe the sun is at the center of (what we now call) the solar system. Nothing about reality had changed; what changed was the shared theory—the view of reality—that people employed to make sense of their experience. Every paradigm includes not only some shared vision of reality but also exemplars (like the solar system) that serve to illustrate that vision in concrete terms.

Thus, *the same reality means something different when looked at differently*, a notion demonstrated vividly by my favorite perceptual illusion, the duck/rabbit picture [see Figure 2.1]. The picture appears to be either a duck or a rabbit, depending on whether you see the two protrusions from the head as a duck's beak or as a rabbit's ears. Most people see one or the other by default, but can switch between them with a little effort. You cannot see both animals simultaneously.

Figure 2.1 – The duck/rabbit picture.
Anonymous illustrator (1892).

The picture proves that anyone can see two divergent images from *exactly* the same reality. As J. T. Fraser put it, "what we see of things is what we know of them; the sun used to be a chariot but now it is a store of hydrogen bombs."[16] More generally, as discussed earlier in this chapter, meaning derives from context. In the historical example, the context was the shared belief in one astronomical theory or the other; in the perceptual example, you provide the context by the mental "frame" you impose on the picture. In that sense, paradigms provide contexts and enable sense making, whether in scientific observations or those we continually make and rely upon in daily life.

Under normal circumstances, a community's paradigm maintains organizational focus and cohesion implicitly, while managing "business as usual" effectively through social reinforcement of its values, rules, criteria, and boundaries.

Scientific publications are a prime example of boundary maintenance: it is nigh impossible to publish a paper challenging a dominant scientific paradigm in a leading journal because the gatekeepers (reviewers and editors) subscribe so thoroughly to that paradigm.[17] Through a variety of gatekeepers, paradigms simultaneously dictate not only which questions are supposed to be asked and answered, but also which questions are *not* allowed. By their nature, paradigms define, exemplify, and enact what *normal* is supposed to mean for their communities of practice.

Inevitably, however, sooner or later, every paradigm encounters disruptions of a magnitude that cannot be rationalized or brushed aside. In science, when important facts are discovered that the existing paradigm cannot account for, a more encompassing theory must be invented to explain both the new discoveries and the older facts. In commerce and society at large, demographic trends and new technologies regularly create opportunities for competitors to disrupt markets with new business models, and to threaten the viability of normal operations for a wide range of organizations, large and small. An obvious example is the paradigm of how and where to sell books, which persisted for centuries until disrupted by the advent of online commerce and Amazon.com.

The social dynamics that sustain paradigms are intrinsically inertial and conservative, strongly resistant to change. So, disruption of a community's paradigm creates a "crisis" that must be resolved. The most common resolution is called a "paradigm shift," in which, one way or another, a new paradigm comes to replace the old. Given the strength of social forces holding the old paradigm together—particularly the commitment of adherents to a coherent set of ideas, values, and practices—a paradigm shift is likely to be an event of historic significance for the members of any community experiencing it.

It should come as no surprise that community paradigms and individual beliefs share important common features:

- Identity, emotional investment, and values – Members of a community identify with the community's activities and invest emotionally in the paradigm that the group adheres to; the group's values are reflected in what the group does and how they do it.

- Binding to X means blinding to Y – Paradigms *bind* adherents to a particular view of reality, including concepts, values, and practices that comport with that perspective; at the same time, they *blind* adherents to alternative perspectives (cf. confirmation bias); *adherents to different paradigms see the same facts and events differently.*

- Powerful resistance to change – Paradigms are maintained by adherents' natural confirmation bias, and by social reinforcement of values, rules, criteria, and boundaries; it takes a disruptive crisis to change a paradigm, and even then, change may not occur; if it does, a new paradigm replaces the old one.

- What *normal* is supposed to mean – A paradigm defines and socially enforces what is supposed to be normal; it tells us what to think and what not to think (the "discipline" of a political party, corporation, church, or sports conference); most of us effectively "live inside" paradigms even as we push back at them.

All of the preceding bullets apply to individual beliefs as well as paradigms. An individual expressing and justifying adherence to her community's paradigm will sound just like an individual expressing and justifying her own beliefs; she will invoke all the same identifications, emotions, arguments, commitments, and critical examples.

The simple difference between them is that paradigms are a group-level conceptual system for making sense of the world of a particular collectivity, while beliefs are an individual-level conceptual system for making sense of the world as experienced by a particular individual. Nevertheless, in practice, individuals within a community of practice often internalize the group's paradigm as if it were an individual belief system, and beliefs of individuals are often so widely shared among class, ethnic, or political groups that they might as well be paradigms. What is most important about both paradigms and beliefs are the properties highlighted in the bullets above.

Finally, after two chapters emphasizing the diversity and subjectivity of perspectives in the social construction of reality, let me bring "brute" physical reality on board. I need to clarify the distinction between *social* factual reality, which is amenable to multiple interpretations, and a brute *physical* factual reality that must be taken at face value because its existence does not depend on our existing to observe and describe it. As John Searle says in *The Construction of Social Reality*,[18] there could be no such thing as social or institutional facts without the prior existence of brute physical facts. His example of a brute physical fact is the existence of snow and ice near the top of Mount Everest. If every human disappeared tomorrow, snow and ice would still be there near the top of Mount Everest. Add to that all the other brute physical facts you can think of. Although Searle might not agree with me, I would also include the factual relationships embodied in the laws of physics, chemistry, and biology (evolution and ecology). The social construction of human reality does not impinge upon brute physical facts in any way.

With this chapter's foundation of how individuals and groups make sense of social reality, we will continue in chapter three to discuss the ways and means by which humans and cultures construct each other.

3

BELIEF SYSTEMS

In chapter two, we looked at sense making at the level of individuals (beliefs) and at the level of groups or communities (paradigms). Different social dynamics are at play at the group level, but the important psychological features of sense making are largely the same at both levels. In this chapter, our focus is on the societal level, at which culture manifests itself in the world at large.

At this level, our individual psyches are enmeshed not only with our immediate experiences, but also with the sense making activity related to keeping the entire state or nation functioning coherently. Social dynamics at the societal level do not override the beliefs and paradigms grounded in local and immediate experience; rather, they add a layer of depth and complexity, with their concern for principles that apply to *everyone*. In particular, this chapter will explore aspects of authority and justification in those social dynamics, including the pivotal role of authority in justifying the status quo.

As we saw in chapter two, meaning derives from context. This principle applies not only to explaining things but also to justifying them. For instance, "two young boys fighting with each other" *describes* an event. Adding the context "they are fighting because they both like the same girl" *explains* the fight as a competition. Adding the further context "she told them she would go steady with the winner" provides the *reason* for the competition, which *justifies* it as a means to a personally worthwhile objective. Justification aims to make something or someone good or right by providing an explanation in the form of a reason, cause, or warrant, which puts it in a context (frames it) as an end in itself or the means to a virtuous end. Describing, explaining, and justifying are three discrete levels of meaning.

Justification is ubiquitous in our lives and fundamental to social cohesion. However, it is so often background rather than foreground—implicit rather than explicit—that we may not recognize how deeply it is woven into our thoughts. We rarely think about justification unless challenged to offer it; yet, if asked, people can always provide some reason for their thoughts and behavior. We all engage from time to time in mental rumination about why we did this or that, and why other people do this or that. Even young children just learning to tell stories intuit the importance of reasons and pepper their stories with them. The casual use of reasons in ordinary speech, without explicit mention of justification, is so commonplace that its presence is generally "under the radar."

Justification is also known by other names. People attempting to explain or justify their own thoughts or behavior, particularly in questionable circumstances, are said to be *rationalizing*. At the societal level, the ongoing process of explaining and justifying traditions, roles, norms, and other institutional habits is called *legitimation*. As we will see later in this chapter, legitimation is fundamental to the cohesion of culture and society.

Belief Systems and Worldviews

Beliefs were introduced in chapter two as manifestations of identity, emphasizing how emotional commitment to beliefs distorts believers' basic relationship to knowledge. As beliefs "shape the mind" of the believer, a similar distortion occurs in the believer's relationship to values. A believer is no longer passive, neutral, or "objective" about particular facts or values. Facts and values are now either *inside* the believer's trusted world or *outside* it; as captured in the "confirmatory bias" meme, believers latch onto stories that fit their beliefs and tend to ignore those that do not.

Beliefs come in all degrees of scope and focus, from the belief that your hometown sports team will do better this year to belief that humanity will survive the climate crisis. Many beliefs relate to each other in nested hierarchies; for example, belief in the value of organic gardening entails beliefs in the values of natural fertilizers, rotating crops, and local distribution of fresh produce. And all beliefs, like the knowledge and values they incorporate, are linked together in our minds as huge networks of interconnections. Given the inherent systemic interdependencies among beliefs, I will hereafter refer to them all as belief *systems*.

Belief systems are the most comprehensive and functionally important of all human sense making and mental organizing structures. If one's culture is the all-encompassing context within which humans construct meaning, one's belief systems are the ultimate mental manifestations of social construction—one's personal take on the culture. All the other topics in this chapter are either components of belief systems or intended to interact with them. All the workings of one's rational mind, including its back and forth with the intuitive mind, are enacted from the standpoint of one belief system or another. *Subjectively, we all live within our belief systems.*

Three kinds of belief systems are known for their distinctive characteristics:

- *Paradigms* are most notable for the extent to which they define and socially enforce what is supposed to be normal for a particular community of practice. But in this respect, and with respect to all the other features of paradigms described in chapter two, they are typical of all belief systems. The same psychological and social dynamics operate to maintain continuity of business models, economic theories, political parties, academic departments, and bureaucracies everywhere. No one with success and influence in business, politics, entertainment, or any other walk of life wants their standard modes of operation disrupted!

- *Ideologies* are belief systems used to legitimate a particular hierarchy of inequality and power in politics and society. Prime examples are neoliberalism and white supremacy, important topics which will receive proper attention in chapters eight and eleven. Ideologies will surface again later in this chapter in a discussion of legitimation.

- *Worldviews* are the most all-encompassing of belief systems, serving as "symbolic universes" for individuals, or for a society as a whole, whether explicitly acknowledged or not. The prime historical examples of symbolic universes are myth, religion, science, and philosophy.[1] In principle, worldviews are broader in scope than theories (which apply to particular domains of life or knowledge) or paradigms (which are shared by particular communities of practice). In practice, however, adherents of broad theories (such as evolution) and ideologies (such as neoliberalism) often seek to expand their scope and promote them as worldviews in professional, social, and political arenas.

A worldview comprehensively explains and justifies a particular way of making sense of the world and your place in it, establishing its legitimacy through a mutually supportive combination of knowledge, values, and authority. Each worldview comprises an entire "world" unto itself, with its own understandings of reality, truth, and morality. America's contested politics provides ample evidence of this phenomenon. How could being vaccinated against COVID-19 become a political football? Because public health mandates were understood as matters of individual freedom within the worldview of Trump followers, rather than as acts of cooperation for the common good, as they were understood within the worldview of most Americans. Thus, choosing to forgo a vaccination as an expression of autonomy was laudable behavior from within the Trumpian worldview, while from within the majority worldview, it was the epitome of selfishness.

Given the inherent diversity of perspectives across and within cultures and nations, multiple worldviews abound, and *contests among conflicting worldviews are inevitable.* Conflicts in beliefs, even within local tribes, are as old as recorded history. Still, the world today manifests an unprecedented degree of uncertainty and complexity, fueled by a breakdown of confidence in traditional authorities, and compounded by accelerating developments in technology, media, and demographics that encourage exposure to a dizzying and disconcerting array of competing belief systems. How does anyone cope with such cognitive and emotional overload?

First, people sort themselves out when they can. Constructing one's identity amounts to sorting through which cultural belief options to embrace. Also, different realms of society operate under different paradigms, and people are drawn to the institutional profiles that appear to best fit their beliefs. Second, many institutions, like schools and businesses, resolve conflicts in beliefs internally, creating incentives and imposing penalties to narrow the acceptable range of beliefs under their control. Third, most individuals are adept at compartmentalizing, which minimizes conflict by limiting each belief system to one part of their life and not others. Finally, although most of us develop some measure of comfort with multiple overlapping identities, commitments, and belief systems, many individuals who cannot tolerate uncertainty and complexity adopt fundamentalist belief systems that meet their needs for certainty and simplicity. I devote an entire section to this topic later in the chapter.

Considering the open-endedness of the human condition, and the multiplicity of belief systems in the world, it only makes sense that the first priority of adherents to a particular worldview, religion, or political ideology is the need to be "right"—to feel thoroughly validated and justified in their beliefs.[2] This need can manifest itself in all manner of selective perception, distorted logic, and tireless rationalization.[3] Meeting this need, each belief system is anchored in an authority which provides reasons why the belief system is right, thereby establishing its legitimacy. Making ourselves right is the emotional dynamic that makes belief systems self-fulfilling. *Belief systems are self-fulfilling because they are self-legitimating.*

The dynamics of belief systems show how far our species' actual behavior departs from the traditional ideal of "rational man," in which rationality promotes decisions that circumvent the distorting influence of emotions. Instead of that, people commit to beliefs, paradigms, and ideologies for intuitive reasons laden with emotion. Then, once emotionally committed, they use rationality to explain and justify how right their beliefs are. Indeed, a good case can be made that the human capacity for reasoning evolved precisely to explain and justify oneself to others.[4]

Recall from previous chapters that we reify and project social reality from our subjective beliefs. All belief systems, including worldviews and political ideologies, appear to their adherents as being about the real world, not about their own subjective map of it. This is profoundly important because such things as political theories, and concepts like "economic man," thereby take on a life of their own. As our beliefs shape our minds, so too do we internalize (live in and live by) our *legitimated* belief systems. In so doing, we become characters in the story we have internalized about how and why the world works as it does, and we live out the lives of these characters.

Given this understanding of the ubiquity and power of our belief systems and worldviews—that our worldviews effectively become our destiny—do we not have the moral imperative to ensure at least that they embody our "better angels"?

Knowledge and Values

Every belief system can be deconstructed into three components—knowledge, values, and authority—which mutually support and confirm each other. The goal of this deconstruction is to better understand each of the components and how they relate to each other inside belief systems.

Knowledge is the sum of changes in a person's brain as a result of learning, exposure, and experience over time, situations, and circumstances. A great deal of personal knowledge is tacit,[5] operating outside consciousness. Certain types of knowledge reap particularly rich dividends because they amplify or multiply the effects of other forms of knowledge. These include "learning how to learn" and the many skills constituting "critical thinking" and "executive function" (the various facets of self-control). Another especially important type of knowledge is about people and life experience, sometimes described as "emotional" and "social" intelligence; I prefer the term "wisdom."[6]

Knowledge subsumes answers to questions of the "what," "when," "how," and "why" varieties, and includes factual information about the range of values and sources of authority in the world. Individuals vary dramatically and consequentially in what they know about, how much they know, how much they read and travel, their range of experience with physical activities, with natural and artificial environments, and with people of different ethnicities and cultures, as well as their degree of openness to new experiences. All these factors of knowledge, experience, and disposition combine to influence which authorities and values individuals choose to identify with. This is the primary way that knowledge affects values: *people can only value those things, ideas, and other people they know something about.* The best way to be sure no one values something is to be sure they know nothing about it.

Values are statements about (or behavior reflecting) *what is important* to an organism, culture, or individual person, relative to some (typically implicit) frame of reference. In general, values can be understood as criteria by which resources should be allocated in one direction or another; specific meanings, as always, depend on context. For example, an individual for whom social justice is important will devote considerable attention, effort, and emotional commitment to activities she judges to advance that cause.[7] A culture that values the fine arts will allocate financial and other resources to promoting them to the public. Most nonhuman animals, in the interest of survival, expend most of their energy finding food to eat and fending off predators. In this book, I use the word "values" to refer to priorities, objectives, and other desiderata of a culture, community, or philosophy; in other words, "what is deemed worthwhile" and "ways to get there."

As discussed in chapter one, differences in values from one culture to another derive mainly from their unique histories, circumstances, and resulting patterns of social relationships.[8]

Likewise, individuals traditionally learned values primarily from their families and friends, together with some combination of public education and religious training, the foremost socially sanctioned institutional sources of authority. Today, however, the world in which many children grow up is dominated by devices connected to the internet, where they are likely to be exposed to values more reflective of hatred, malice, and greed than faith, hope, and charity.

Different belief systems strongly encourage or discourage particular activities or experiences. For example, many state boards of education prohibit public schools from teaching "the theory of evolution." This directional effect on behavior is the primary way values influence what one knows about, and therefore what one might come to value. Conversely, acquiring significant new knowledge and experience—for example, with the natural world, or with people of different ethnicities and cultures—can profoundly affect one's values.

A conventional shibboleth is that facts and values are distinct categories; for example, that facts are empirical, while values are not. Particularly strong is the stricture that one cannot derive a value-laden "ought" from a factual "is." But we see here how *knowledge and values are interdependent and tightly coupled;* specifically, that beliefs and paradigms dictate which aspects of reality we see (and which we do not), so what counts as knowledge depends in large part on values (embedded in beliefs and paradigms). Ironically, this relationship illustrates the extent to which "is" actually derives from "ought"! The facts versus values dichotomy is at best naïve, if not just plain false.

Authority and Legitimation

Authority, a unique and distinctive aspect of all cultures, is defined as *power* to influence or command thought, opinion, or behavior.[9] Authority may be vested in a person, a position (or bureau), a document, a practice (or ritual), or an ideology. In combination with knowledge and values, authority is the component of belief systems that gives them legitimacy. We endow the knowledge and values of a belief system with rightness and validity because we trust or identify with its authority component. For example, people who followed public health advice to be vaccinated against COVID-19 without hesitation did so because they trusted (the authority of) the science supporting the advice.

From an organizational perspective, authority is the power to make decisions which guide the actions of another—a relationship between two individuals, one "superior" and the other "subordinate."[10] Superiors have the right to issue commands and subordinates perceive an obligation to obey. What distinguishes sanctioned authority from coercion and force, on the one hand, and from persuasion and social influence on the other, is perceived *legitimacy*. According to Max Weber's classic typology, the three basic sources of legitimate authority are: the legal system, including constitutions, laws, and regulations; history, norms, and traditions, including hereditary monarchs; and extraordinary personal charisma, including religious figures.[11]

Why does authority have power to influence us? Where does its power come from? Since authority is a species-wide phenomenon, humans must inherit some instinctive disposition to divide ourselves into leaders and followers. This disposition almost surely derives from the fundamental relationship between all mammal parents and children: *all mammal offspring are born needing to be taught by their parents how to function in the world.* At some level, this disposition toward authority is baked into all humans. The parent-child (superior-to-subordinate) relationship is the metaphorical archetype for authority in all human cultures.[12] In Western cultures, the two most common ideals of authority are the "strict father" paradigm and the "nurturant parents" paradigm. The former emphasizes unquestioned obedience while the latter focuses on caring and support, but both paradigms presume and rest squarely on a parental superior-to-subordinate relationship.[13]

Differences between the strict father and nurturant parents paradigms of authority map directly onto the crucial distinction between absolute and legitimate authority. *Absolute authority* is based on domination maintained by brute force or the threat of it. Prototypes of absolute authority are kingdoms, slavery, and colonialism. Less pure examples are authoritarian dictators, criminal syndicate bosses, and strict fathers who demand unquestioned obedience from their children. Dominated subjects are powerless. Absolute authority is justified by a belief in a natural order of things in which the authority is higher on the metaphorical ladder and naturally superior. It is "legitimated" by the benefits alleged to accrue to subordinates, but always with the condition that subordinates must obey orders whether they like it or not.

In contrast, *legitimate authority* occurs when *subordinates* understand and rely on the benefits that flow from the relationship with their superiors, and therefore *willingly* grant them authority. Legitimate authority is like a partnership with reciprocity, rather than domination. The political embodiment of legitimate authority is participatory democracy, in which responsible leaders are freely elected by informed constituents. Legitimate authority also characterizes organizations that choose leaders regularly, classrooms with student-centric teachers, and families whose parental control systems derive from nurturance rather than dominance.

In practice, *it is rare to find either absolute or legitimate authority in pure form, but the distinction between them*

is fundamental to the moral weight of legitimate authority.
Authority is not truly legitimate unless subordinates *internalize*
the value of the relationship. Monotheistic religions are a
good case in point. To a follower without faith, these religions
exemplify absolute authority vested in all-knowing, all-powerful
Gods and their earthly spokespersons. Followers achieve great
benefits from community membership and meaningful rituals,
but unquestioning obedience is demanded in return. A follower
who proclaims faith in her religion, however, announces that she
has internalized the entire belief system and willingly granted
it legitimate authority. No wonder faith is virtually the defining
characteristic of monotheistic religions.

Moral authority is the genre of authority trusted specifically
to know right from wrong and good from bad, and to make right
and good decisions. It is the capacity to convince others *how
the world should be*, as opposed to *how the world is* (the latter
is "epistic" authority). Moral authority justifies and legitimates
which set of knowledge and values shall be operative. Each
comprehensive belief system is a package including knowledge,
values, and the rationale for itself. Believers attach to the whole
package, but it is the moral authority that anchors the belief.

Until the mid-twentieth century—and in many circles even
today—the premise underlying claims of moral authority was
that there exist fundamental truths, either metaphysical or
religious, independent of the moment and even written laws,
which dictate normative principles for behavior. Given the
persistence of multiple competing worldviews, however, moral
authority will always be contested and needs its own justification.
*The ultimate moral issue is which authority should be trusted to
decide the answers to normative questions.* This entire book can be
read as justification for the moral authority of natural humanism.
I make the case for natural humanism directly in chapters six and
eight, and somewhat more expansively in chapters nine through

eleven. For now, however, let me just mention some parameters and criteria of moral authority relevant to its justification.

The two defining parameters of moral authority are its source (Is it natural or supernatural?) and its functional model or metaphor (Is it strict or nurturant?). Concerning its source, moral authority must be grounded in something superordinate—bigger, older, or wiser than ordinary mortals—and the only sources that qualify are either supernatural (imaginary) beings or the natural world itself (of which humans are a subordinate part). As for the functional model, there may well be options other than strict or nurturant, but these two are the most common and will suffice until a contender emerges.

I divide the justification criteria for moral authority into two classes, universal ones and those specific to the focus of this book. The universal criteria are transparency and accountability, which seem self-explanatory. Why should one trust a source of moral authority without transparency and accountability? The criteria that arise from the premises of this book are *pluralism* and *openness*. As explained in chapter one, the inherent multiplicity of norms, values, and perspectives across cultures compels a pluralist approach to morality and legitimate authority. Openness is a second paramount criterion because it encourages new experiences and acknowledges that circumstances are always changing. I will say more about both these criteria in the final section of this chapter. I should add here that democracy as a process, fully implemented, meets all four of these criteria very well, most likely accounting for its unique moral status.

The process of *legitimation* has been mentioned throughout this chapter, as it is so thoroughly implicated in belief systems. We have seen, in particular, that legitimation plays an active role in belief systems by leveraging authority. In combination with knowledge and values, each belief system is anchored in an authority which provides *reasons why the belief system is right*, thereby establishing its legitimacy.

The need for, and provision of, a steady dose of reasons why our beliefs (and behaviors) are right and good is ubiquitous at the individual, community, and whole society levels. The same emotional dynamics are operating at the personal identity level, the community paradigm level, and the whole society worldview level. As circumstances change, our attachment to personal and institutional habits of thought and behavior is persistently subject to threats, challenges, and new opportunities. There may be no limit to the repertoire of excuses, rationalizations, and really good reasons that humans will employ to maintain an even keel against the winds of change.

Thus, at the societal level, the purpose and effect of legitimation is to maintain the role of a particular belief system in a political or institutional regime, or to maintain the domination of a particular belief system against the threat of a rival to it. In both cases, legitimation is the essential process that keeps the belief system viable (not unlike the role of homeostasis in organic viability, as we shall see in chapter five). Finally, it is worth noting that legitimation *as a process* is morally neutral; it serves the same function whatever the regime: to reinforce the status quo on an ongoing basis, and to sustain ongoing institutional habits across generations. When propaganda is used by ideologues to legitimate a particular hierarchy of inequality and power, however, there is nothing morally neutral about it!

Uncertainty and Fundamentalism

Humans have no intrinsic limits as to how we construct belief systems. As previously noted, this open-endedness is at once liberating and frightening. For most of human history, for most people, the frightening side of the equation has been by far the most salient. If anything goes, how to tell right from wrong? Doubt, fear, terror, and despair are the words most often used to describe this pervasive aspect of the human condition. Histories of myths and religions always recognize the role of all-encompassing belief systems in assuaging existential fear and despair.

It is important to connect the dots between these ubiquitous existential fears and the relentless intellectual striving since the dawn of Western civilization to intuit or discover absolute, ultimate truths about reality—the striving famously characterized by John Dewey as "the quest for certainty."[14] This disposition extends from scientific theories (universal laws) through religious dogma (the word of God) though the more general notion that there must be One Right Answer to any question. The common thrust of this cultural imperative is to dispel *uncertainty*, an emotional state that can be intolerable for many people. The practical effect is to create a huge disconnect between official theory, dogma, or sanctioned expertise and most people's daily experience, which is filled with the actual complexities and internal contradictions of postmodern society.

Today we understand that *reality is complex*, beyond full comprehension. Truth demands multiple perspectives; there could not be one right answer for every question because each question is more or less connected to any other question. In most every human endeavor, we find ourselves reconciling competing objectives. Our whole legal system rests on a history of cases in which competing arguments are weighed against each other. Parenting necessarily includes continuously attempting to reconcile the conceptual complexities and conflicts of principles that societies and cultures construct to make life livable.

The complexity, internal contradictions, and increased rate of change characteristic of postmodern society can only be managed by a kind of mental gymnastics that many individuals and entire cultures fail to master. Many people around the world feel threatened by the changing circumstances of their lives. And many politicians are all too ready to exploit these feelings by characterizing other people (minorities or immigrants) or different points of view as threatening.

As a result, we see all around us a direct connection between the *perception of threat* and the adoption of fundamentalist belief systems.[15] As Heinz Pagels wrote, "the characteristic of all fundamentalism is that it has found absolute certainty—the certainty of class warfare, the certainty of science, or the literal certainty of the Bible—a certainty of the person who has finally found a solid rock to stand upon which, unlike other rocks, is 'solid all the way down.'"[16]

Among paradigms and belief systems, what distinguishes fundamentalism is its characteristic rejection of diversity of opinion relevant to its established "fundamentals," along with a purist delineation between members and nonmembers of the group. All paradigms tend to close the minds of adherents to other perspectives, but not all paradigms or belief systems are grounded in the *certainty* of their principles.

Fundamentalism projects the internal convictions of the individual into the objective external world as a form of certainty *about the world*.[17] When this certainty revolves around the perception of threat from other people, or from other points of view, fundamentalist belief manifests itself as an active, aggressive opponent of pluralism, democracy, and any hope of constructive evolutionary change in culture or world affairs. In Pagels' words, "fundamentalism ... is a terminal form of human consciousness in which development is stopped, eliminating the uncertainty and risk that real growth entails."[18]

In the context of the doubt and uncertainty intrinsic to the human condition, fundamentalism is a completely understandable part of human sense making, yet history and the present time prove it to be a potentially fatal *design flaw*. As we approach planetary limits and global interconnection, fundamentalism threatens our very survival. The constructive alternative is to replace the flawed system of belief that fuels and props up these feelings with more open-minded alternatives.

Accountability and Pluralism

In concluding Part I, I wish to address two important issues that first surfaced when I introduced naturalism and pluralism as basic premises of natural humanism. The *naturalism* premise denies the legitimacy of any supernatural or transcendent source of truth or morality.[19] However, human culture—including all human belief systems—belongs to the natural world. So, inventing supernatural explanations of human affairs certainly qualifies as natural behavior. Is that a contradiction? The second issue is whether the *pluralism* premise implies the equivalence of all points of view. Are we not left with moral relativism? My attempt to clarify both issues follows.

There is no doubt that human behavior is part of nature; nor is there any doubt that humans have imagined supernatural and transcendent beings and places for as long as human history can be recalled. Moreover, hundreds of millions of people are true believers in religions based on faith in supernatural or transcendent beings. These people and their belief systems are surely a major, significant part of the natural world.

The issue here, however, is the *legitimacy* of supernatural or transcendent sources of authority on matters of truth and morality—whether these sources should be trusted to decide these matters. The argument rests on the criteria for legitimate authority, and whether or not supernatural or transcendent sources meet these criteria. Accountability is the only criterion we need to consider.

A few pages ago, I asked rhetorically, "Why should one trust a source of moral authority without transparency and accountability?" Here, the pertinent question is, how can one question or challenge anything supernatural or transcendent?[20] Legitimate moral authority requires accountability, as exemplified in a relationship of responsibility between leaders and followers. But the essence of supernatural and transcendent sources of authority is to be above and beyond dispute. In fact, followers of supernatural and transcendent authorities are expected (or required) to accept their decisions *on faith*.

Faith in entities and leaders whose decisions cannot be questioned or challenged may suffice for legitimacy in a worldview grounded in absolute authority, but it does not meet the accountability criterion for legitimate authority in a world of multiple competing worldviews. Absolute faith in any authority precludes accountability. Without accountability, the teachings of the authority are never tested, never measured against brute facts or potentially competing knowledge or values. Adaptation to changing circumstances is hindered, if not entirely stifled.

This provides a fitting segue to our second issue: Does pluralism imply the moral equivalence of all points of view? To answer this question, we need to break it down into two parts: the moral or normative part, and the knowledge or "epistic" part. Pluralism is fundamentally a response to an epistic issue, *the inherent incompleteness of all points of view*. As spelled out in chapter one and the previous section, truth (brute facts excepted) demands multiple perspectives. We need diverse points of view not only to home in on the truth but also to have confidence in the process of truth-seeking and hence in its results. The normative issue of moral relativism arises because this epistic resolution strikes at the heart of the belief that there is one right answer to every question, including (or especially) moral ones.

The very idea of diversity and multiplicity is contradictory and threatening to anyone whose worldview tilts toward homogeneity—oneness, unity, and assimilation of differences. This worldview should be instantly recognizable as the long-standing American political approach to immigration and enculturation of ethnic (and religious) diversity. This antipathy to diversity is one of the core issues dividing American politics today.

The rub is that multiplicity, variety, and diversity are epistic necessities because they are basic biological and social facts. The more we see continuity between biology and culture, the more we understand humanity as *part of* the natural world and not *apart from* it, the more we need to recognize diversity as a core truth of any sustainable belief system. I will develop this argument further in chapter eight and the remainder of the book.

The equivalence of all points of view is a straw man. Everyone has their own belief systems, which necessarily favor certain values (and therefore points of view) over others. Natural humanism offers two general principles—two types of criteria—that clearly delineate the normative consequences of various viewpoints. The first one is the necessity of multiplicity and diversity as core truths, for both epistic and normative reasons. The normative concern is the inherent multiplicity of norms, values, and perspectives both within and across cultures, which compels a pluralist approach to morality and legitimate authority.

The second general principle is open versus closed systems of thought and policy. This principle is also derived from biological and social facts. As described in chapter five, all living systems, including human cultures, are open systems. Life is always adapting to changing circumstances. Any system of thought or policy that is not open to new experiences and changing circumstances is a dead-end street that can only make sense in an authoritarian political regime with no concern for the planet or humanity.

Summing Up (Part I)

Humans are generally more impulsive, irrational, and self-deluding than we would like to think we are. This characterization is nothing new; philosophers and playwrights have beaten these drums for centuries. What is really new, and extremely important, is understanding that we are not so much inheritors of a "given" world as *creators* of it. This understanding is so important because of how *empowering* the constructionist paradigm is.[21]

Our forefathers co-constructed and co-evolved the world we inhabit today. In so doing, they believed their goals and values were timeless. Yet they never anticipated today's global interconnectedness, nor planet Earth's ecological limits to unconstrained growth of the fossil fuel industry. Now we face a crisis that requires writing a whole new script, including a new set of goals and values to transform our way of living in a hurry.

The constructionist paradigm is one fundamental building block of natural humanism. Understanding our role as co-constructors of our own belief systems energizes us to take on the challenges ahead. It is most certainly in our power as a species to transform our way of life to adapt to the threat of climate change *if we can make up our minds to do so.*

We now turn in Part II to a detailed description of humanity's place in nature—the complementary foundation of natural humanism—and to the resulting case for the natural world as the essential source of moral authority in the current century.

PART II

HUMANITY IN NATURE

The interconnectedness of things, the reflection of one in another, shines with a clear light that the coldness of eighteenth-century mechanism could not capture.

— Carlo Rovelli (2021)[1]

In Part I, we established that humans effectively live in our own self-constructed belief systems, each one providing its own version of the truth. From this pluralistic vantage point, traditional, universal moral absolutes from ultimate authorities no longer make sense. We also saw that moral authority must be conceptually grounded in something super*ordinate*, and that super*natural* sources are inherently unaccountable. By these criteria, the natural world emerges as the only entity superordinate to humanity that could plausibly qualify as a legitimate source of moral authority.

I think there are other good reasons to consider Mother Nature as our moral guide. First, the natural world is our species-wide collective home. In this respect, it enjoys unique status as the universal context within which all of humanity can work together to make sense of moral and political issues. Second, the natural world has been regulating itself sustainably for eons, and we are the ones whose collective behavior has already begun to disrupt planetary health. To put it bluntly, the larger natural world has figured out how to operate sustainably, and we have not.

For these reasons, I propose we look to our natural world as the fount of values and guides to action. To this end, the following chapters examine humanity's place in nature. Rather than the entire universe, our focus will be on its most relevant aspect, life on Earth. While the universe encompasses far more than our singular planet, Earth is the proximate context for understanding ourselves as a biological species.[2] The counterpoint to our biological humanity is our cultural humanity, also an interconnected part of life on Earth.

The purpose of Part II is to explain how biological/cultural humanity relates to the whole of life on earth. The familiar approach to this subject tells the story of how humans evolved from ancient organisms through precursor primates, and how human social and economic structures evolved from ancestor hunter-gatherers to today's post-industrial economy. This evolutionary perspective is absolutely necessary but not sufficient to address questions about what human goals and values should be. My approach is complementary, emphasizing how living systems in biology and living systems in culture operate by the same rules and principles as each other (except when humans willfully break the rules!). The essential role and significance of evolution is never far afield, but my primary goal here is to spell out the functional parallels between human civilization and life on earth as a whole.

Part II consists of four chapters: "Systems Thinking" provides the conceptual vocabulary for describing nature's (and humanity's) dynamics. "Living Systems" describes how organisms stay alive by remaining coupled to their environments, and the principles underlying evolution and adaptation in the face of continually changing conditions. "Humanity's Relationship To Nature" argues that we should construe the relationship as humanity's subordination to nature, so that humanity's biological dependence on the health of the biosphere becomes a cultural moral imperative. Finally, "Life's Healthy Operating Principles" draws on the preceding chapters to extract a set of principles that keep nature healthy, and considers the relevance of these principles to human values and practices.

4

SYSTEMS THINKING

There is no ultimate or perspective-free way to describe nature, only a choice among perspectives best suited for one purpose or another. Our goal here is to understand the place and role of humanity in nature. As we shall see, a Systems view of nature is the best approach for this purpose.

Contrast with Mechanistic Paradigm

In the (conventional and familiar) mechanistic scientific paradigm, the large-scale architecture of the Universe is portrayed as innumerable clusters of galaxies, each containing innumerable individual galaxies, of which our own Milky Way is one. Our sun is one of innumerable stars in the Milky Way. Our sun and its planets constitute the solar system. Of these planets, the third closest to the sun is our home, Earth, the only (known) place in the Universe where life exists.

The primary focus of the mechanistic paradigm is objects. Each object (in the universe) is not only a "whole" consisting of smaller parts but also a part of some larger whole. (The term "holon" was invented to capture this duality.)[1] Looking down the biological hierarchy, each human body is a whole object consisting of organs, which consist of cells, which consist of cell components, and so on down to smaller and smaller parts.

Looking up the social hierarchy, individual humans are parts of families, which are parts of tribes or communities, which are parts of towns or cities, which are parts of states or nations, which are parts of the whole of global civilization.

Central to this older paradigm is the belief that "the whole is the sum of its parts." Mechanistic explanations aim to show how higher-level features of a whole entity arise solely from its parts and their interactions. It is assumed that the properties of the whole entity are caused by its parts and their interactions. This is the principle and practice of "reductionism," which seeks to explain any complex phenomenon by *reducing* it to (nothing more than) something simpler or more fundamental.

The Systems viewpoint is an entirely different paradigm. It stands in relation to the mechanistic paradigm like Quantum mechanics stands in relation to Newtonian mechanics: it adds depth, insight, and universality without making mechanism in any way wrong or useless. The Systems view provides a context for understanding Nature within which mechanistic truths play a different role and assume a more limited status. The physical and chemical laws of matter and energy are no less valid; they simply provide *incomplete* (necessary but insufficient) explanations, and are therefore less centrally important.

In the Systems view, the large-scale architecture of the Universe is an infinitely vast web—*a network of interconnections* among systems from the subatomic level of organization to the metagalaxy level. This hierarchy of levels is based on the achievement of stability at larger and larger scales. Each level higher in the hierarchy includes the systems at all lower levels. A system's stability reflects the fact that its internal structure can maintain itself as conditions both inside and outside itself change. In this book, we are concerned only with the intermediate levels in this hierarchy, from chemical molecules at the lowest level of organization to world (global) systems at the highest level. This is the scale of *life on earth.*[2]

A system, then, is any set of things *interconnected* in such a way that they produce and sustain their own pattern of behavior over time. A sports team remains a sports team even when all the personnel change, as long as the hierarchies, purposes, and incentives remain the same. Your body replaces its own cells regularly without any noticeable consequences. Systems of any complexity are inherently more than the sum of their parts.[3] [4]

Feedback Processes

The basic unit in systems thinking is a *feedback process,* which entails the bedrock concept of *circular causation,* where the output of a process feeds back to regulate the input. Consider the classic example[5] of filling a glass of water: From the familiar viewpoint of *linear causation,* the statement, "I'm filling a glass of water" construes you, the actor, causing the water level to rise. In fact, however, as you fill the glass, you monitor the gap between the current water level and the desired water level [see Figure 4.1]. You adjust the faucet position to slow the water flow as it nears the desired level, turning it fully off when the glass is full.

Figure 4.1 illustrates the five-variable "water regulation" *system* you are operating. The variables are organized in a circle of cause-effect relationships, constituting a feedback process operating *continuously* to achieve its goal.

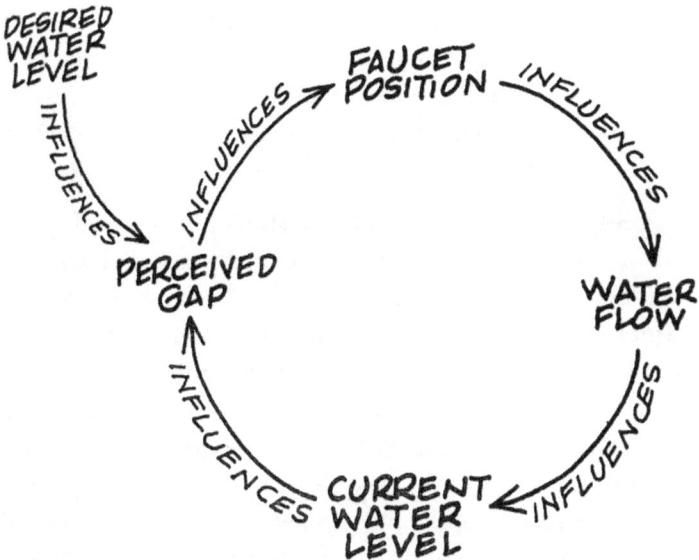

Figure 4.1 – The "water regulation" system used to fill a glass of water. Adapted from Senge (1990) p. 76

Linear thinking implies one-way causality: *you* cause the water level to rise. But this is only half of the feedback process, from "faucet position" through "current water level." It is equally correct to describe the other half of the process, that the "current water level" controls your hand ("faucet position"). Both descriptions are equally incomplete. The full causal story is that *your intention* to fill a glass of water *initiates a system* that causes water to flow until the glass is full. Your brain ("perceived gap") and hand ("faucet position") participate in the action, but it's the (specific, interconnected) structure of the system that causes the outcome.

In Figure 4.1, a prototypical control system, the desired water level serves as the *reference value* of the water regulation system. Although one or more reference value(s) are fundamental to the operation of any control system, in *complex* systems, the reference values for control systems at lower levels of the whole system typically originate as outputs of other, interconnected systems at higher levels of organization. In the simple case of Figure 4.1, your intention to *fill* a glass of water—the desired water level—supplies the reference value.

Feedback processes are of two distinct fundamental types: "balancing" and "reinforcing." Goal-oriented behavior is controlled by *balancing* (or stabilizing or "negative") feedback. Examples are filling a water glass (as above) and controlling the speed of a car with your foot on the accelerator as you monitor the speedometer. A thermostat controls room temperature using the same logical structure; the human role is to set the reference value for the system. (It's called negative feedback because the system operates to *reduce* the gap between a signal value and a reference value.) Goal-oriented control systems, structured as they are to achieve or maintain an externally-provided reference value *as conditions vary*, are intrinsically intentional and purposive.

Reinforcing (or amplifying or "positive") feedback processes are engines of growth. The social network Facebook, for example, becomes more valuable to everyone when more people participate in the network, and this amplifying effect keeps growing more and more without apparent limit. So-called virtuous and vicious cycles, like falling in love and escalating anger—in fact, all *self-fulfilling* dynamics—are other instances of reinforcing feedback processes. Notably, so is free-market capitalism, as it purposefully rejects the stabilizing effects of social norms or regulation.[6]

Hierarchical Levels

A familiar example of hierarchical levels is a personal computer (or smartphone). In brief, the (lowest) hardware level includes a central processing unit and input and output devices, coded to perform low level functions (e.g., logic, arithmetic) so that an operating system can be built "on top of it." The operating system level provides system-wide functions (e.g., graphic display, network connectivity) as well as software tools for applications to be built "on top of it." The applications level provides more specific tools (apps) which enable diverse users to achieve a variety of individual goals.

The higher levels in a hierarchical system could not exist without the lower levels. In any contiguous pair of levels, the functional properties of the lower level both *enable* and *constrain* what systems at the higher level can do. A lower level is often described as a "platform" on top of which higher-level functions can be performed. For example, users don't need to know anything about the operating system to run an application. You don't have to know the details of how an automobile works to be able to drive one. A basic principle of all *control* hierarchies is that higher levels tend to appear simpler than lower levels by hiding irrelevant details.

Higher levels of a system typically influence lower levels by specifying goals or reference values for them (so-called "downward" feedback or causation). A mundane example is a boss telling subordinates what is expected of them. In the personal computer example, you—as the higher level in the control hierarchy—can use an application to specify the "settings" which customize the operating system to work to your liking.

In complex artificial systems, humans *intentionally* design lower-level functions to enable higher-level functions. In nature, complex systems evolve over time from interconnected stable configurations of simpler systems (stable intermediate forms). Intentional or not, new functional properties *emerge* at each new level of organization, properties that originate *only* when the simpler parts are assembled in a particular way. Emergence is an enigma from a reductionist perspective because the new functional properties are *intrinsically unpredictable* from the properties of the simpler parts themselves. Emergent properties at higher levels are *not* caused by the lower-level components; they are caused by the combined effect of the specific *pattern of interconnections* among the components. In short, *emergent phenomena are system properties.*

Let me circle back to clarify the role of physics and mechanism in the systems viewpoint of nature. The simple and essential fact is that all physical (as opposed to symbolic) systems incorporate materials and mechanisms into their structure to achieve their goals. A thermostat can serve its function only because of how the system is organized, but the component parts are mechanisms. The human heart is a seriously complex system, but its essential function of pumping blood is completely mechanical. The planet-wide ecosystem of all life on earth—the biosphere—fully incorporates rocks, air, and water (inorganic physical materials) as integrated resources at all levels of life. The laws of physics are not repealed; they are universal enablers of, and constraints on, what systems can do. And a mechanistic view remains aptly explanatory of the function of any material system component.

Even today, a great many scientists subscribe to the mechanistic paradigm of nature. In their minds, the only path to truth is through component analysis and reduction. It is long past time to knock that paradigm off its pedestal. To comprehend nature's dynamics relevant to life on earth and the human condition, the systems viewpoint is a necessary corrective to the historical dominance of the mechanistic paradigm. As it supersedes mechanism, the systems paradigm also provides an alternative to a reductionist approach to truth about nature. From the systems viewpoint, truth resides in those patterns and relationships that recur across all levels of reality, such as cycles of causation, limits to feedback processes, and the interdependence of the whole network of life on earth (cf. the science of ecology). The main takeaway from this summary of systems thinking is that reduction to physics is not sufficient to illuminate life on earth. Instead, as Gregory Bateson insisted, to unlock the mysteries of life and mind, we must look for "patterns that connect."[7]

5

LIVING SYSTEMS

Even the simplest organisms exhibit organizational features for which there are no non-living counterparts.

– Terrence W. Deacon (2012)[1]

To do full justice to the subject matter of this chapter would require at least a semester college course, perhaps many more. For our purposes, it suffices to focus selectively on the principles of living systems most directly relevant to humanity's place in nature. I begin with what single-celled organisms need to survive; how they succeed in doing that; and the related critical dependencies. These dynamics apply to all living systems, biological and social alike. Then I consider how life evolved from single-celled organisms into the entire self-regulating biosphere of planet Earth, and identify the processes common to all adaptation, development, and control systems. Finally, I look into increasing complexity, diversity, and self-regulation in ecosystems throughout the biosphere. Human civilization fits neatly into this picture.

Metabolism and Homeostasis

All living things—from single-celled organisms to human communities—have capacities, perform functions, and achieve purposes that set them apart from nonliving things.[2] *Self-maintenance* is the most basic of these functions, without which none of the others is possible. What's true of a single cell is no less true of the most complex living systems: despite constant flux and change within and outside the cell, it manages to maintain its own structure, dynamic balance, and individuality. How does this happen?

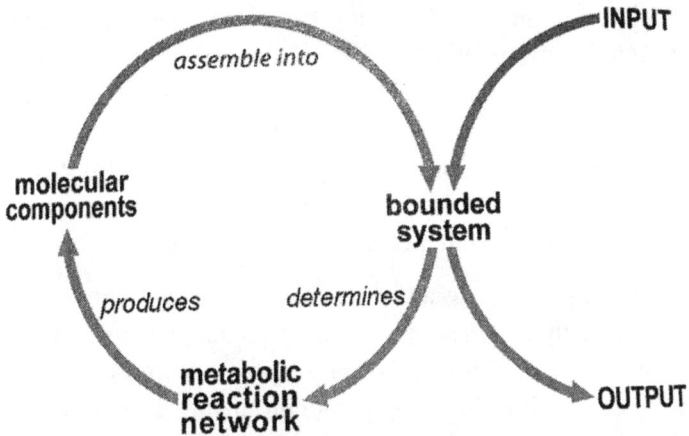

Figure 5.1 – The circular logic of cellular life.
From *The Systems View of Life* by Fritjof Capra and Pier Luigi Luisi
© Fritjof Capra and Pier Luigi Luisi 2014. Reproduced with permission of the Licensor through PLSclear

Cells achieve self-maintenance through a complex set of interconnected processes following the circular logic illustrated in Figure 5.1. Each cell is organized as a *bounded system* that determines a *network of chemical reactions* which produce *molecular components* that continually assemble themselves into the (very same) *bounded system*. This orchestrated set of metabolic processes repeats endlessly. This system is *open* to its environment, transforming its *input*—nutrients and energy outside its boundary—into the chemical reactions inside its boundary, while returning the resulting waste products as *output.* What's profound about this system is that the cell is literally making and remaking itself! As Capra and Luisi put it, "Life is a factory that makes itself from within."[3]

The structural distinction between "open" and "closed" systems is important. Like the cell shown in Figure 5.1, all *open* systems interact with their environment by operating on sources of energy or information that flow into and out of the system through its boundary. Thus, on the input side, humans breathe air, eat food, drink water, and convert those materials into bodily needs; on the output side, we sweat, pee, and poop, returning waste products to our external environment. The staff of a daily newspaper "ingests" and filters scores of potential stories, turning some into published items in a persistent structure and discarding the remainder in the dustbin of history.

Closed systems may also interact with their environment, but only indirectly. In a *closed* system, external energy or information sources must first be coded (transformed) by sensors within the system before they can operate on them. Thermostats, for example, require an internal component that can sense and encode ambient temperature. Notably, all biological nervous systems interconnect with other systems within the bodies they occupy, but they can interact with the world outside the body boundary (e.g., skin) only through the sensors and effectors of that body.[4]

Metabolism is the term denoting the entire network of enzyme-catalyzed, life-sustaining chemical reactions in all organisms, from single cells to human beings. Metabolism achieves three main functions: the conversion of food to energy that runs all the cellular processes; the conversion of this fuel into the structural building blocks for proteins, lipids, nucleic acids, and some carbohydrates; and the elimination of wastes. Without successful ongoing metabolism, organisms lack the energy to maintain their structures, grow and reproduce, and respond to their environments. *Metabolism is fundamental to life itself.*

The cell membrane—the boundary between the cell's inner and outer environments—is operationally part of the interior architecture of the cell. Its critical function in metabolism is to control which ions and molecules are allowed to pass into and out of the inner environment. The cell membrane must "know" how to serve this function, as every control subsystem in every organism must "know" its vital reference levels. This information is either encoded in genetic instructions or it is set dynamically (in real time) by one or more signals from interconnected subsystems at higher levels of organization.[5]

In complex organisms like humans, the skin is the organ that plays the analogous biological boundary role for the whole person as the cell membrane does for single-celled organisms. Humans use sense organs (including touch, embedded in the skin) and lungs and digestive organs to interact with the external world. Boundaries (and borders) are also critical components of all social systems, from clans to communities to companies to nations. All social systems define a boundary between insiders and outsiders. They must have methods of adding new members from inside or outside the boundary, and methods of rejecting or isolating persons who don't fit the requirements of insiders.

No living thing exists without a matching environment. Organism and environment are two sides of the same coin. *All organisms require their inherited surroundings always to be there* to provide critical levels of the energy and nutrients they need to survive. All living systems have a *tolerance range* of reference values within which they must remain or else become destabilized. A living system suffers or degrades as its environment diverges from optimum. We all know what happens to humans denied oxygen or water for longer than their bodies can tolerate. Similarly, all social and cultural entities require an adequate level of resources to sustain themselves. College courses disappear when enrollment drops below a specified level or "outside" resources are reduced. TV shows without audience share are canceled.

Nevertheless, for all living systems, the normal state of affairs is a flux of continuously changing environmental conditions. In single-celled organisms, it is the cell membrane that *regulates* the flow of molecules into and out of the cell's internal milieu, ensuring that all the chemical parameters necessary for life are maintained in their respective critical ranges as environmental conditions fluctuate. These vital ranges are called *homeostatic*, and the process of achieving the dynamically balanced state for all these chemicals is known as *homeostasis*. For humans, despite changes in environment, diet, or level of activity, the list of variables that must be maintained within homeostatic range includes body temperature, fluid balance, the pH of extracellular fluid, concentrations of sodium, potassium, and calcium ions, and blood sugar level. According to the distinguished neuroscientist Antonio Damasio, homeostasis is the essence of "life regulation."[6]

Metabolism is the vital set of *energy* processes; homeostasis is the vital set of *regulation/control* processes. Homeostasis and metabolism work in tandem as the fundamental integrated energy and control systems necessary for life maintenance. Homeostasis achieves its regulatory functions in part by controlling rates of metabolism. Both vital processes require a complex web of interconnections among myriad feedback processes to achieve their purposes.

Another process fundamental to living systems, cell division, occurs in one of two ways. Somatic (non-reproductive) cells divide by *mitosis*, the process whereby a single cell divides into two complete replicas, each containing the full complement of chromosomes. The new cells are what cause organisms to grow, as well as what enables them to continually replace old or damaged cells, self-repair being essential to self-maintenance. Cell division by the process of *meiosis* creates female egg cells or male sperm cells, each with half the number of chromosomes of the parent cell; this is the mechanism behind genetic diversity in all sexually reproducing organisms. Cells regulate their own division through a network of protein-mediated feedback processes (control systems), which can sometimes be modulated by interactions with the environment.

Adaptation, Emergence, and Autonomy

A theme running through everything said so far about living systems is *adaptation*: the act or process of achieving a better fit for a specific or new use or situation, typically with some modification or adjustment involved in achieving the better fit. A broad and abstract concept, adaptation can be achieved by many different kinds of systems at all levels of size and complexity. As examples so far, adaptation is accomplished by variations in *metabolism* at both the cellular and the whole organism level, in that the external supply of nutrients and energy is in flux, yet the network of chemical reactions can stabilize and maintain the production of molecular components. It is achieved by *homeostasis* in each instance of a variable maintained despite changes in environment, diet, or level of activity, as well as in the entire process of life regulation. Cell division is adaptive in replacing old or damaged cells, keeping all parts of the organism intact. Likewise, programmed cell death is adaptive in removing damaged cells. And in the process of growth, the entire body must adjust its proportions and relationships as new cells are added.

There is far more to life than adaptation, but the dynamic is ubiquitous in living systems. Evolution and individual learning, to be discussed ahead, are different types of adaptive processes from the ones described so far. From the lowest level of cell self-maintenance to the highest level of evolution at the planetary level, adaptation is on the short list of life's fundamental characteristics.[7]

Descriptions of what keeps organisms alive and healthy can be re-framed as descriptions of what protects them from vital threats. Living systems die if their internal milieu is not maintained within critical levels; thus, homeostasis is the first line of defense against many deadly internal threats. But specialized systems have evolved to protect against other dangers. Most organisms have some kind of innate *immune system* that helps to protect them non-specifically from microbial pathogens. Jawed vertebrates took a step up the evolutionary ladder to develop *adaptive* immune systems, in which exposure leads to immunological memory. Besides learning to fight off diseases from bacteria and viruses, human immune systems form the first line of defense against many early forms of cancer. And during early stages of development, most embryos or fetuses with critical abnormalities are naturally aborted.

One way cultural systems are inferior to biological systems is that threats to the vitality of political and economic institutions often exceed critical thresholds before people recognize the need for protective systems.

In the complex system of reciprocal synthesis and organization that constitutes life, the components are not "parts" from an engineering perspective. Each component of any living system, including each individual cell, is kept alive by its own internal network of metabolic and homeostatic feedback processes. The whole, integrated process of life *emerges* from the combined, coordinated effect of multiple interconnected energy and control subsystems working cooperatively across different levels (the whole system being interactively coupled through its boundary with its environment).

Even at the level of a single cell, all living systems manifest *autonomy* in that they determine for themselves what their structure will be. This autonomy is one aspect of life's most distinctive feature, its organization as *a system that literally makes itself*. This distinctive type of organization is called "autopoietic" (self-forming); the self-making *process* is called *autopoiesis*.[8] Another aspect of autonomy is the organism's being an operationally closed system, in that it contains everything it needs to be itself within its own boundary. What it needs and takes from its environment are nutrients and energy.

Being alive, as Terrence Deacon writes, is "intrinsically historical and dynamic. Being alive does not merely consist in being composed in a particular way. It consists in *changing* in a particular way. If this process of change stops, life stops, and… the cells and molecules distinctive to it immediately begin to degrade."[9] Life keeps itself going dynamically. Like a burning flame, if a living system is deprived of the oxygen it needs, the dynamic process stops—and life expires.

Evolution

How did life evolve from single-celled organisms into the entire self-regulating biosphere? The core ideas of *variation* and *selection* were first highlighted by Charles Darwin in the mid-nineteenth century. Darwin's goal was to account for the origin of *species*, meaning *populations* of organisms consisting of similar individuals capable of interbreeding. Darwin asked, How could one species ever beget a new and different one? What kind of process could ever produce that result? Long before anyone knew how biological inheritance might work,

Darwin assumed the existence of some such mechanism. He proposed that "descent with modification" created *variation* within the species population. Then, over time, after one or more reproductive generations, some of these variations would persist while others would not. Darwin proposed that the persisting variations would be the ones better *adapted* to the particulars of their environmental niche; in other words, the variations which *fit* their environment better. Thus, the phrase "survival of the fittest" became the motto for Darwin's principle of Natural Selection, a truly revolutionary idea.

After more than a century and a half of overwhelming empirical support for evolutionary theory, there remain significant differences among scholars in many of the nuances and implications that may be drawn from the theory. The core concepts of variation and selection, however, are as solid and robust as any in science, albeit understood today as broader and deeper than in Darwin's initial formulation. The original idea of random variation in the gene pool, conceived early in the 20th century, is now understood to encompass *all sources of novelty, creativity, innovation, and variation* that are replicable, including not only chance mutations but also symbiosis (microbes in the human gut, babies, and parents), partnerships, cooperation, and other synergies (emergent interdependencies), as well as countless forms of cultural innovation (such as artistic expression and disruptive business or political practices).

No matter the source, neither biological nor cultural evolution can occur without novel possibilities contending for some ecological niche. This is one reason for the intrinsic importance of *diversity* at all levels of nature and society. *Without sources of novelty and variation, there can be no evolution.*

Darwin's original concept of fitness has also been updated and expanded. Selection means choosing among varied candidates according to specific *fitness criteria*. Not only does each ecological niche manifest unique fitness criteria, but also these conditions are constantly in flux (the more so as climate change accelerates). Species that cannot adapt or evolve quickly enough to keep up with changing environmental conditions are forced to move geographically if possible or else become extinct.

Moreover, we now understand that both biological and cultural selection operate concurrently at multiple levels of organization. From single-celled bacteria causing human infections to cultural memes circulating on social media, variation and selection occur not only among individuals, but also among families, groups, tribes, communities, teams, companies, and nations. For example, each team's locker room has a different "culture" representing its own ecological niche. Players new to a given locker room quickly learn how to adapt their behavior to its fitness criteria.

As times change, the fitness criteria for success in human cultures change with them. Novel ideas or inventions competing for attention and persistence are subject to the mercurial fitness criteria of the current Zeitgeist (as filtered by media publishers). Ultimately, as we saw in chapter three, ideologies and other belief systems are the most consequential fitness criteria in human societies. "Living" inside a belief system can effectively block reception of competing ideas, unless one of its core beliefs is to remain open to new ideas, if not to continually seek them.

Biological reproduction requires some kind of *persistent storage* for genetic instructions like DNA. In genetic reproduction, if instructions are replicated without error, each replication is a perfect copy. If replication is imperfect, variation occurs. Whether the result of a given replication event happens to be continuity or change, persistent storage of repeatable instructions is required for living systems to reproduce (and all persistently stored information is inherently susceptible to modification).

Indeed, *persistent and modifiable information storage plays an essential role in adaptive processes found everywhere in nature.* Persistent storage enables adaptive behavior in a variety of ways, as illustrated by the following three different kinds of adaptive processes: self-maintenance, biological evolution, and learning.

- In the case of self-maintenance, described earlier, organisms retain their distinctive structure and individuality despite the flux of conditions both external and internal to them. In this kind of adaptation, ongoing disturbances are accommodated by homeostatic and other kinds of control systems without changing the organism's basic structure. Feedback cycles are on the order of hours. The specific structural pattern maintained by the organism's control systems is encoded in the persistent storage of the organism's DNA molecules. All living systems manifest this kind of adaptive behavior.

- Biological evolution is a different kind of adaptive process, in which a *population* of organisms becomes better suited to its habitat. The persistent storage medium is the same DNA molecules with a much longer feedback cycle, at least one reproductive generation. The main difference in kind is that the variation occurs in a series of iterations over time, rather than in a continuous process. Moreover, the selection criteria are applied not to the genetic instructions themselves, but to the *results* of those instructions, the fully developed organism at the age of reproduction. This is the broadly important distinction between an organism's *genotype* (the original network of genetic material) and its *phenotype* (the eventual organism, as developed and transformed by life circumstances). The phenotype is the subset of the genotype as expressed in the organism. For DNA to be passed on, its phenotype must meet the selection criteria because *selection occurs at the level of phenotype, not genotype.*

- Individual and cultural learning are other kinds of adaptive processes, in which experiences and their outcomes lead to modifications in persistent storage structures. Learning shares with evolution the basic pattern of a series of iterations over time; in the context of learning, the process is often characterized as "trial and error." By learning to do more of what works and less of what does not, the brain modifies itself, and cultural institutions modify themselves, to adapt to changing circumstances.

The common thread in these three kinds of adaptive processes is how the *information* preserved in persistent storage enables adaptive behavior across a wide range of contexts and time frames. In the words of John H. Holland,[10]

Though we readily ascribe internal models, cognitive maps, anticipation, and prediction to humans, we rarely think of them as characteristic of other systems. Still, a bacterium moves in the direction of a chemical gradient, implicitly predicting that food lies in that direction. The repertoire of the immune system constitutes its model of its world, including the identity of "self." The butterfly that mimics the foul-tasting monarch butterfly survives because it implicitly forecasts that a certain wing pattern discourages predators. A wolf bases its actions on anticipations generated by a mental map that incorporates landmarks and scents. ... *the behavior of a complex adaptive system stems from anticipations based on its internal models [emphasis mine].*

Cognitive maps and internal models extend the range and effectiveness of living control systems; the information in these maps and models adds specificity and nuance to any decision process. Recall that systems at lower levels make decisions and take action toward goals specified by systems higher in the control hierarchy. For example, we might experience mental conflict were a lower-level system to get "mixed signals" from a higher level of our mental apparatus, which would occur if more than one map or model were in play at the same time. We learn early on by trial and error to refer such conflicts to an even higher mental level for resolution.

Virtually all the essential attributes and patterns that define life are present in the simplest of organisms. The functions and capabilities of single-celled organisms are a combination of two different kinds of processes, both essential. First are core survival processes of self-definition, self-maintenance, self-repair, and self-regulation, exemplified by metabolism and homeostasis. These processes allow for a *limited* range of deviation from *optimal* environmental conditions. Second are open-ended, flexible adaptive mechanisms that direct development[11] through a series of stages, each of which prepares the organism for the next stage. The singular quality of these *adaptive* processes is that they allow development to proceed under a wider (but not unlimited) range of inner and outer circumstances.

One consistent evolutionary trend is for living systems to develop more and more complex and sensitive adaptive capabilities. Advanced adaptive capacities, the combined result of networks of control systems and internal maps and models, greatly extend the scope of external conditions organisms can accommodate. Outstanding examples include adaptive immune systems, which apply learning principles to defend an organism against unpredictable pathogens; the plasticity of nervous systems, which recruit other available neural tissues to replace a function previously served by damaged neural tissues; and human language, the epitome of an open-ended symbolic system. The ultimate example of advanced adaptive capacities must be the human brain, which has evolved into a limitless mapmaker and model-builder of the physical, social, and symbolic worlds in which we live. Of profound consequence, the human brain also maps and models *imaginary* versions of those worlds.

Another consistent evolutionary trend, at the level of populations and ecosystems, is increasing diversity. The evolutionary dynamics of variation and selection have operated for *billions* of years, generating *astronomically high* instances of novel possibilities for *unimaginably diverse* fitness criteria to match. This creative process has produced a living world that never ceases to amaze and humble us in its diversity, complexity, and beauty. One of evolution's iconic patterns is the tree of life, depicting a wide diversity of species as finer and finer branches spreading out from the ancestral trunk.

Diversity is both a cause and an effect of evolution. As a cause, it helps ensure sufficient variation of possibilities for fitness criteria to act upon. In human terms, any brainstorming process benefits from a diverse group of ideas. As an effect, diversity (within species, among species, and among ecosystems) ensures a robust capacity to survive change. Some seedlings survive a forest fire better than others. Some aquatic life will survive the current glut of plastic better than others. Some humans have a natural resistance to diseases that others don't.

Non-Determinism and Control Systems

Not only are all living systems intrinsically autonomous, goal-directed, and adaptive, but they are also *dynamic* and *non-deterministic*. (Events are non-deterministic if they cannot be predicted precisely from prior conditions).[12] As mentioned earlier, all *open* systems operate on sources of energy or information that flow into and out of the system through its boundary. Homeostasis ensures that all the internal chemical parameters necessary for life are maintained in their respective critical ranges as environmental conditions fluctuate. Each parameter has a critical *range* rather than a fixed value, enabling organisms to function normally under (some range of) fluctuating conditions. As long as they continue to import sufficient energy from the environment, open systems remain in "non-equilibrium." Rather than settling into a *static* state of chemical equilibrium, living systems fluctuate around states (collections of chemical parameters) that define their *dynamic* steady states.

This dynamic quality is one aspect of an organism's being non-deterministic. Humans are not predictable for many reasons, but one of them surely is that everyone is a "different person" from one day to the next. You can never tell how even your closest friend is going to be feeling the next time you see them. We all have "good days" and "bad days." These are manifestations of (among many other factors) fluctuations within the normal, acceptable range of our homeostatic parameters. All organisms have a limited but *dynamic* range of conditions under which they can function and a limited but *dynamic* range of potential behaviors.

Non-determinism also inheres in the fundamental difference between genotype and phenotype. All organisms begin life with an inherited network of genetic instructions (the genotype), which was once assumed to be deterministic. But selection occurs at the level of phenotype, not genotype. Recent decades of research in molecular biology have identified many pathways, systems, and mechanisms by which *an organism's life experience feeds back information to its genes, thereby affecting their expression.*[13] Outcomes of the genotype's initial ensemble of possibilities depend definitively upon ensuing conditions. The time passing between inherited possibilities and actual outcomes is filled with all the unpredictable circumstances of development and subsequent living that every organism encounters. Thus, *evolution creates new possibilities, but it does not determine which of them will prevail.*

All living systems act (if only via chemical reactions) to reduce discrepancies between current perceived states and internal reference states. This is the basic unit of a control system, whose reference state we colloquially call a goal or purpose: the "end" state that makes sense of why an action occurs. In human affairs it's self-evident that actions are motivated by objectives, desires, and intentions; not only those of individuals, but also of teams, companies, and nations. The same is true of all of biological nature, right down to the level of a single-celled organism. Plants operate by the same action-with-purpose control systems, lacking only locomotion. The feedback/control cycle as the basic functional unit of living systems means that goal-seeking, purposive, *intentional causation is an attribute of being alive.*[14] [15]

The fact that all *life* is inherently purposeful is another way to say that living systems are organized and structured to keep themselves alive. The overriding purpose of being alive is to stay alive, which of course implicates and subsumes many subordinate goal-driven processes, such as metabolism, homeostasis, and reproduction, each of which must be successful for life to persist. This imperative to stay alive is the root source of all "biological value"[16] and intentionality. The imperative to stay alive is also the root of the phenomenon we call the "will to live." Living organisms don't die until a necessary body function stops working. In humans there is evidence that the will to live can keep a person alive who would otherwise die, at least for a day or two,[17] indicating powerful top-down feedback control over vital functions by the highest levels of brain function. We may safely assume that all living systems manifest this same kind of "will to live."

Nevertheless, the fact that life is inherently purposeful does *not* imply that the evolution process has any goal, intention, or purpose of its own. Evolution surely has its own *logic* (variation and selection), and time has proved this logic applicable to all living systems, including human civilization. The logic of evolution has unrivaled potency; and the process of evolution is ubiquitous (and may incidentally serve the purposes of some segments of society from time to time). But there is no evidence that evolution has its *own* purpose. That said, and as mentioned earlier, evolution does manifest at least two consistent *trends* over time: populations and ecosystems become more diverse; and living systems develop more complex hierarchies of organization and control.

Complex hierarchies manifest three basic types of causal feedback processes: "upward" causation, "downward" causation, and mutual constraint. An example of *upward* causation is ideas or beliefs spreading from neighborhood groups to public officials, who pass them on to influence their peers in local government, and so on up through county, state, and national levels. This kind of influence is also prevalent within biological systems. Almost everything in the human body is connected to everything else through hundreds of brain nuclei. For example, a signal of discomfort from an internal organ can easily disrupt your attention, mood, behavior, and thinking. As for *downward* causation, described earlier, a physical example is consciously inhibiting a sneeze or cough, and social examples include managers telling their reports what their goals or targets are, or legislators passing laws that become constraints on their constituents' behavior.

Mutual constraint—another basic type of causal feedback process—occurs whenever living systems communicate reciprocally with each other; for example, in family interactions. Spouses are bound together in relationships of mutual constraint. So are children and their parents. The same parents relate by mutual constraint with their own parents, as well as with their work commitments. A person you hire to do a job around the house is constrained by your parameters, as you are constrained by theirs.

We are all mutually constrained by each other when we behave according to cultural *norms*, which constitute an extremely effective cultural self-regulation (control) system. The entire fabric of über cooperation that holds civilization more or less together functions as interconnected networks of mutual constraints. And to be sure, the very same kinds of elaborate networks of reciprocal relationships operate to regulate and sustain biological ecosystems.

Ecosystems

An ecosystem is a community of organisms in a particular physical environment. Ecosystems extend the functional unit of "single organism coupled to its environment" to the unit of "community of organisms coupled to a collective environment." Large numbers of organisms sharing the same space all adapt to each other over an extended period of time. Individual organisms retain their autonomy as self-maintaining and self-regulating systems, but the individual organism systems are nested organizationally within the ecosystem. Being part of a community adds a new level of complexity and mutual constraint in both biological and social ecosystems.

As open systems, biological ecosystems maintain a flow of energy into and out of their location. Green plants play a pivotal role in this process. Their roots take in water and mineral salts from the earth to be transmitted to the leaves, where they combine with carbon dioxide from the air to form sugars and other organic compounds, including cellulose, the main structural element in cell walls. This process of *photosynthesis* is the basic energy factory for all the planet's biological ecosystems.[18] Photosynthesis converts solar energy into chemical energy bound in organic substances, and releases oxygen into the air to be recycled by other plants and by animals through respiration.[19]

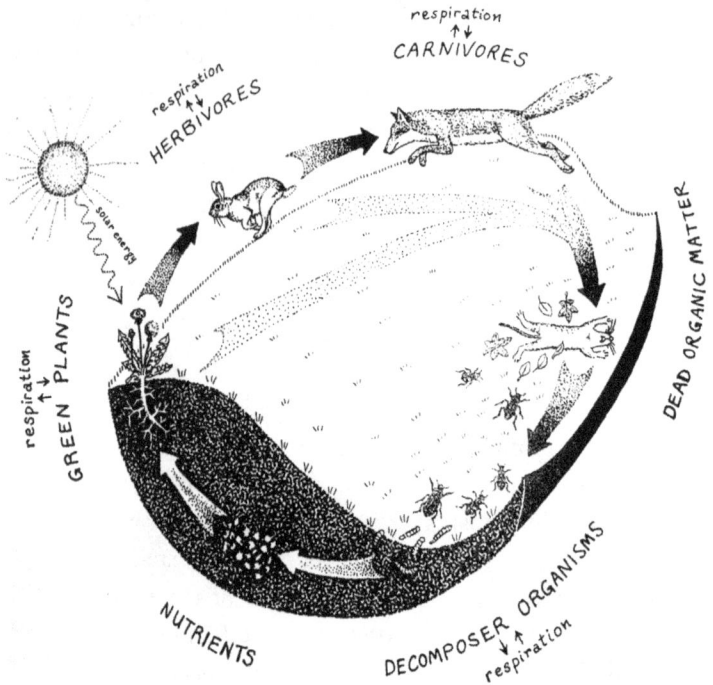

Figure 5.2 – A typical food cycle.
Adapted from Capra (1996) p. 179

Figure 5.2 depicts a typical food cycle, greatly simplified. As plants are eaten, their nutrients pass on through herbivores to carnivores, while energy dissipates through respiration and excretion. Excrement, as well as dead animals and plants, are decomposed by insects, bacteria, and fungi, which break them down into basic nutrients, to be taken up again by green plants. The food cycle exemplifies the principle of recycling. Because waste for one species is food for another, the only waste generated by the ecosystem as a whole is heat energy from respiration, which radiates into the atmosphere and is replenished by the sun through photosynthesis.

Biological ecosystems range in size from a single rotting log to an entire ocean.[20] Really large ecosystems—regional communities of plants and animals extending over a few square miles or more—are called *biomes*. The global sum of all ecosystems is the *biosphere*, which incorporates the earth's rocks, oceans, and atmosphere. The biosphere encompasses all life on earth; it reaches up in the atmosphere roughly 5 miles, where vultures and geese may fly, and to ocean depths of nearly 7 miles, where a variety of life forms have been found.

At any scale, ecosystems are exposed to constant external fluctuations and disturbances, such as variations of rain, wind, and temperature from day to day, and from one season to the next. Ecosystems self-regulate for the same reasons and in the same manner that individual organisms do. For organisms, the range of values of vital chemical parameters must remain within homeostatic limits. Ecosystems, located in geographically bounded areas, have an additional, different kind of limit to consider: the maximum population (of one species or another) this environment can sustain indefinitely, considering not only the food, habitat, water, and other resources available in this location, but also the environment's ability to handle accumulations of waste products and other destructive factors. This limit is called the ecosystem's "carrying capacity." Ecosystems continue to self-regulate as a population threatens to exceed their carrying capacity, but exceeding this limit causes a breakdown. Scientists have been warning us for decades that

Earth's carrying capacity for the human population is roughly 9-10 billion.[21]

The whole of Earth's biosphere self-regulates. Evidence is conclusive that the chemical composition of Earth's atmosphere evolved in tandem with life's evolution, and that Earth's surface temperature has remained at a level comfortable for life for about four billion years, even as heat emanating from the sun increased by about 25% during that time. However, the Gaia hypothesis, first proposed by chemist James Lovelock and co-developed by microbiologist Lynn Margulis in the 1970s, goes much further. Named after the Greek mythological goddess who personified Earth, the Gaia hypothesis posits that Earth is a self-regulating system involving the biosphere, atmosphere, hydrospheres (oceans), and pedosphere (rocks and soil), tightly coupled as an evolving system that operates through feedback processes to achieve *planetary homeostasis*. In the words of Lynn Margulis:

> Simply stated, the [Gaia] hypothesis says that the surface of the Earth, which we've always considered to be the *environment* of life, is really *part* of life. The blanket of air—the troposphere—should be considered a circulatory system, produced and sustained by life. … Life actually makes and forms and changes the environment to which it adapts.[22]

Here, we can only scratch the surface (pun intended) of the Gaia hypothesis. Over the years the hypothesis has been formulated along a continuum of weaker and stronger claims, and the stronger claims continue to generate degrees of criticism along a continuum of earth scientists, some of whom still carry reductionist torches. In a word, the Gaia hypothesis is controversial.

One need not believe planet Earth is fully alive, however, to picture Gaia as a living system. James Lovelock himself suggested the analogy of a tree's trunk.[23] The only living cells around the perimeter of a growing tree are in the thin layer of cambium beneath the bark. All the wood inside is dead. Likewise, Earth is covered with a 10-12-mile-deep layer of biosphere; the living part of Gaia is like a thin film around the planet. A tree's bark protects the cambium from damage, as the atmosphere shields life from harmful factors (such as ultraviolet radiation) and helps regulate terrestrial temperature. Neither the atmosphere nor the pedosphere (rocks and soil) is alive, yet both participate in the planet's self-regulation system, like the bark and wood of a tree.[24]

More on The Human Condition

In this chapter, I have focused selectively on aspects of living systems most directly relevant to humanity's place in nature. Two broad generalizations about living systems strike me as especially significant to the human condition. First, *organisms and their environments are so tightly coupled as to be essentially one unit.* Everything alive is a system in which an organism or ecosystem is coupled *interactively* with its environment. Coupled interaction is shorthand for "a control system of interconnected feedback processes, regulating the flow of energy (biological systems) or the flow of symbolic communication (cultural systems) back and forth between organism and environment."

Every organism is born ready to couple with a particular kind of environment. That environment is *literally* an extension of the organism, without which the organism does not exist. Organisms depend on their environments for life itself. This relationship is true of all bacteria, mammals, ecosystems, human cultures and institutions, the whole biosphere—of every living system, at all scales. Humans are not made to live alone. Some humans do live alone, of course, but individuals cannot achieve their full humanity without other people—our cultural environment—because so many social needs and capacities are built into our genetic inheritance as social animals. Earth's atmosphere is the "environment" of the biosphere. Atmosphere and biosphere interact continually, mutually constructing each other; in particular, in regulating the relative amounts of oxygen and carbon dioxide in the atmosphere.

There are two stages involved in fully grasping the meaning of this coupling. One stage is to know something about the dynamics of metabolism and cell membranes, to be able to picture at a molecular level what it means to be alive and breathing. This information is what most educated people in the United States are exposed to in primary school. The second, deeper stage is to "get" *the (circular-causation) concept of the intrinsic interdependence* of organisms and their environments, as described in this chapter—the same concept described in Part I in relation to humans and their cultures. A major goal of this book is to achieve this stage of understanding.

The second significant generalization about living systems is that the physical and chemical environment of life is continually changing, epoch-to-epoch as well as moment-to-moment. This truism about reality is why the multiple types of adaptation discussed earlier are so fundamental to living systems. *To be alive is to be always adapting to changing circumstances.* Environmental fluctuation is continual at every time scale. Natural things are always changing, in constant motion, like a tree branch bending with the wind. For organisms to survive in the face of constant change, long-term as well as short-term, they must evolve more and more robust (diverse) and flexible adaptive systems. This result is just what nature's fitness criteria produced through biological evolution.

The existential necessity to adapt to changing circumstances has a stark implication for human civilization. On the one hand, individual human beings are blessed with brains capable of learning about and adapting to anything we can map or model (as well as what we can imagine) in our minds—perhaps the paragon of flexibility. On the other hand, humans' emotional needs and cognitive biases have resulted in cultural, economic, and political institutions that strongly resist change—a very strong bias toward stability.

Humans are every bit cut from the cloth of biology and evolution, where the existential dilemma of stability versus flexibility has been playing out for billions of years. Our emotions generally favor stability over flexibility, continuity over change, and (the illusion of) security over (the perception of) risk. Our belief systems actively engage in self-perpetuating rationalization. At this time in our species' history, as the climate crisis begs for prompt and comprehensive change, it remains an open question whether humans will be able to summon the collective vision and political will to adapt our civilization constructively in time to avert biological collapse.

With that thought, we turn a narrative corner from mainly factual, functional content about living systems in this chapter— call it "descriptive" material—to a series of "prescriptive" chapters. The next two chapters map what we know about living systems into two different frameworks. The immediately following chapter considers the issue of humanity's relationship to nature. Given what we know about the human condition and living systems, how should we construe this relationship? In the chapter following that one I discuss how various principles contribute to the health of the biosphere: "Life's Healthy Operating Principles." These principles, in turn, will play a major role in the subsequent development of a naturalist morality, the centerpiece of natural humanism.

6
HUMANITY'S
RELATIONSHIP TO NATURE

Humanity relates to nature in myriad ways, but this chapter is concerned with only one question, How *should* we construe the relationship of humankind to the Earth's biosphere? To be clear, there cannot possibly be one best, timeless, ultimate way to answer this question. The best we can aspire to is a coherent, useful, and timely answer at this moment in history, when humanity faces a climate crisis and urgently needs a species-wide vision for how to cope with it.

I begin by describing the relationship I see from an ecological perspective. Then I focus on the essential difference between the ecological and conventional perspectives, as well as other reasons why the ecological worldview is opaque and problematic for so many Americans. Finally, I return to the topic of moral authority as discussed in Part I to consider the benefits of understanding and embracing the idea of ourselves as *totally dependent on* nature's health for our existence and survival.

Our Biological Selves and Our Cultural Selves

Ecologists are scientists who study interactions among living systems and their environments. To think ecologically is to think holistically, in systems terms, about how everything in the living world interconnects and relates to everything else. In the last chapter, I reached the conclusion that every living thing is a system in which an organism or ecosystem is *coupled interactively* with its environment. Organisms and their environments are so tightly coupled as to be essentially one unit. No organism or community of them can stay alive without its coupled environment. This relationship holds at all scales of living systems, from bacteria to the entire biosphere, whose environment is Earth's atmosphere.

What does such an interactively-coupled relationship of ecosystems to environments mean for humanity? Humans are both biological and cultural selves. Our biological selves live in biological ecosystems like every other community of organisms. We are inextricably bound to nature for our very existence. Humanity is integrated with nature the same way our hearts and lungs are integrated with our bodies. Biologically, we are completely *dependent* on the health of the biosphere for our survival.

Our cultural selves, meanwhile, live in *symbolic* ecosystems. Our current social, political, and economic institutions have evolved from what our founding fathers invented to fulfill the goals and aspirations of their era. America has always embraced a wide range of beliefs about what our collective goals should be. As a result, our enduring institutions are built on some widely shared bedrock assumptions, like the rule of law, allowing them not only to maintain day-to-day stability, but also to include mechanisms to accommodate varieties of opinion and changing circumstances. In particular, our Constitution specifies a government with checks and balances among its three branches, while also providing for its own continuing amendment, exemplifying how to achieve both stability and flexibility at the same time.

Nevertheless, as brilliant and foresightful as the U.S. Constitution may have been, no one in the 18th century could possibly have anticipated the magnitude and scope of change humanity has experienced since then. Although our fundamental human condition remains the same, the industrial economy has transformed the Earth's biosphere beyond our wildest imaginations. And although the founding fathers would still recognize the shape of the country they set in motion, the insights and perspectives of cognitive, cultural, and ecological science that inform this book did not even sprout seeds until early in the 20th century. Now, a century later, humanity finds itself torn between the raw facts of the global climate crisis, which cry out for immediate and systemic change, and intensive efforts from myriad vested interests to maintain the status quo.

For our cultural selves, tight coupling between beliefs and institutions presents both challenges and opportunities. Because belief systems and institutions are so *interactively* coupled, neither side of the dynamic can change significantly without forcing the other side to adapt by changing in tandem; beliefs and institutions effectively control each other. Given the climate crisis imperative to change direction, the main challenge we face is how fiercely individuals and institutions resist pressures arising from changes in belief, to the point of covering up and denying facts, and of spreading misinformation and propaganda to deny a toehold to new demands. The opportunities are the flip side of the challenge: even small *institutional* changes in new directions will promote further changes in belief, creating positive feedback loops to accelerate further individual and institutional change, above and beyond what now seems attainable.

It is long past time for our cultural selves to be sensibly aligned with our biological selves. The ideologies used in the past to justify exploitation and destruction of nature are now threats to our survival. We must replace such outmoded conventional thinking with a proper, timely, and actionable view of ourselves in relation to nature. This view should be anchored in the realm of moral authority, specifically in the understanding of humanity as *totally dependent on* nature's health for our existence and survival. I will pick up this thread again after an interlude to examine the premise of conventional thinking that clashes most directly with ecology, and a few other reasons that the ecological worldview is especially difficult for Americans to accept.

Earth Does Not Belong to Humans

The essential core of conventional thinking about humanity's relationship to nature is the idea that *Earth belongs to humans.*

For about 25 *centuries*—from the dawn of Western civilization in ancient Greece through the middle of the 20th century—conventional wisdom and Biblical authority[1] have held that humans have the right and obligation to exploit nature and all its resources for their benefit. This vision entails both metaphysical and moral claims: that in reality, humans are *separate* from nature, and also that humans are entitled and obliged to exploit all its resources. Science has essentially, if implicitly, been on the same page. Traditional scientific method requires observers to assume an *objective* (neutral, outsider, or "God's eye") viewpoint toward any subject; and formally, only research conducted from an "objective" perspective counts as real science.

Moreover, all contemporary economic theories treat costs inflicted on nature as an "externality," removing all connections with and impacts on nature from economic calculations concerning any public or private decision or policy. In practice, then, *the three most dominant Western cultural paradigms— religion, traditional science, and free-market economics—presume that humans are separate from nature (and entitled to exploit it)*. This relationship is never questioned in mainstream culture, politics, and economics; it is a foundational premise, completely taken for granted.

The idea that *Earth belongs to humans* has another slant: that humans are *in control* of the planet. This belief adds an additional assumption about our power: that humans are not only entitled to exploit the earth, but also capable of correcting any problematic consequences. Our role is to "manage" the earth, and thus to make our own trade-offs concerning how much population growth or oceanic pollution we will tolerate. Either the market will take care of it, or someone will intervene technologically to correct any problem that arises. As one telling example of this mindset, for decades, the environmentalist movement adopted the stance that it was humanity's role to "save the earth."

However, as Naomi Klein observes,[2] this perspective is backwards and upside-down:

> *When we…resolve to save the planet, we cast ourselves in a very specific role. That role is of a parent, the parent of the earth. But the opposite is the case. It is we humans who are fragile and vulnerable and the earth that is hearty and powerful, and holds us in its hands. In pragmatic terms, our challenge is less to save the earth from ourselves and more to save ourselves from an earth that, if pushed too far, has ample power to rock, burn, and shake us off completely.*

Despite being fundamentally misguided, it is hard to overstate how emotionally laden, and well-entrenched this conventional view is, that *Earth belongs to humans*. It has such a long history, is so entwined with our politics and economy; and yet it is only one piece of the puzzle. The gap between ecological thinking and the American version of Western thought is perilously wide. Here are a few examples:

- The exploitative mindset of *Earth belongs to humans* (aka extractivism) is intertwined with the practical imperatives of free-market capitalism to grow and expand without limits. Whereas regulation (stabilizing control systems, homeostasis) is fundamental to all living systems, the very concept of regulation of human choices has been anathema to American capitalism from its inception. It is impossible to reconcile unconstrained exponential growth with an ecological worldview.[3] [4]

- Most Americans live on a treadmill of overconsumption, fueled by total saturation in targeted advertising. Americans eat too much (unhealthy) food, buy too many disposable goods, and pay high prices for self-indulgent conveniences. Some individuals voluntarily engage in ecologically-conscious behavior (conservation, reuse, and recycling), but even significant incentives in that direction fail to dampen wasteful consumption by the vast majority of Americans. Downshifting the all-American lifestyle of overconsumption will be a steep uphill climb.

- Because many Americans are taught from childhood to think of everything in terms of linear causation, the ecological concepts of circular causation and mutual construction can be real stumbling blocks for them. Similarly, a heavy emphasis on analytic modes of thought—modes that emphasize parts over wholes— means that holistic and systems thinking can also be challenging for most Americans. Thus, for traditional thinkers, which means many Americans, the reality of human contribution to climate change can seem totally opaque, and hence easy to reject or ignore.

- Compared with the citizens of other Western countries, Americans are extreme individualists. In market theory, prices are set by the abstraction of independent individual choices. In political theory, collectivities are conceived from the perspective of individuals who make commitments to be governed. The whole is always (reductively) conceived as arising out of the interests of, and/or for the benefit of individuals. Radical individualism regards "government" regulation (or any enforcement of constraints or sanctions) as taking something away from individuals.

Combining hard-core individualism with a libertarian philosophical orientation, many Americans cannot abide any form of constraint on their freedom. Yet unconstrained freedom is the opposite of how nature works. In nature, autonomy and self-expression are prevalent among organisms. But *relationships* of parts to the whole are always constrained by preeminent needs at the higher level; feedback regulation through downward-causation control systems prevents actions of parts from disrupting needs of the whole, or individuals from exceeding the range of acceptable community behavior.

Considering the breadth of mainstream American beliefs flatly contradicting an ecological perspective, we can see why the climate crisis has developed to this point without an appropriate sense of urgency. The facts are clear, but dominant American beliefs provide no way to make sense of them. People are emotionally attached to paradigms blinding them to the extent of irreversible damage the industrial economy continues to do to the biosphere. To see these patterns and dynamics would require a dramatic shift in consciousness. Facts alone will never produce that result.

To me, the most intractable tension is between the climate crisis imperative—to embrace the basic role of constraints in the natural world—and the prevalence of targeted advertising with the message, "you are entitled to anything you want." Americans are constantly bathed in media reinforcing unconstrained desires. If any future civilization will require at least a somewhat more constrained approach to life, what could possibly persuade this audience to get on board?!

The Moral Authority of an Ecological Mindset

I believe the climate crisis should be framed to be understood in the context of *moral authority.* This approach has the unique benefit of combining emotional heft with *normative* efficacy. We need not only to overcome inertia and active resistance to an ecological mindset, but also to provide a compelling framework for collective commitment to ecological goals. My rationale follows.

Begin with the premise that, in reality, the climate crisis poses an existential threat to the survival of humanity. This threat is universal—species-wide—not local to any culture, nation, or region. And it is already imminent; there is no escaping it, not even for the billionaires among us. Such an imminent threat to all of humanity is literally without precedent. *What could be of higher priority than to secure our survival?* If we could chart a course to avoid extinction, would we not all rally to its cause? If we could agree that our survival depends on the achievement of a certain set of goals, how could we not all be ready to sign up for them?

The perspective of ecology provides the model of humanity in nature that illuminates the path. In brief, human survival depends completely on maintaining *the health of the Earth's biosphere*, so humans should immediately redirect our energies toward restoring and sustaining nature's health. The maintenance of the biosphere's health can be distilled into a set of principles (such as interdependence, recycling, and self-regulation) which will be discussed with specificity in the following chapter, "Life's Healthy Operating Principles." The single most direct and effective way humanity can restore and sustain biosphere health is by living sustainably ourselves.

It follows that, to secure our survival in the face of the climate crisis, *our entire species should make its highest priority the achievement of "life's healthy operating principles."* This common objective *should* take precedence over all outstanding differences in ideologies and policies among nations. It is often surmised that the only thing that can overcome entrenched differences among nations is a superordinate threat to them all (say, hostile aliens from outer space). Well, extinction of our species from climate change certainly qualifies as a superordinate threat!

The question remains, how to overcome the extensive obstacles to mainstream acceptance of the ecological perspective while also providing an enticing framework for collective commitment to ecological goals. The answer is that *moral authority* supplies the necessary ingredients.

Recall the distinction between *absolute* and *legitimate* authority. Absolute authority claims and asserts domination maintained by brute force or the threat of it. The mindset that *Earth belongs to humans* is a clear instance of superordinate domination and absolute authority of humans over the planet. In contrast, *legitimate* authority occurs when *subordinates* understand and rely on the benefits that flow from the relationship with their superiors, and therefore *willingly* grant them authority. Authority is not truly legitimate unless subordinates *internalize* the value of the relationship.

What we aspire to do is convert current adherents to the absolute domination of humans over Earth into ecologically wise citizens who willingly grant legitimate authority to nature's healthy operating principles. The really heavy lifting is to convert obsessively entitled consumers into somewhat self-restrained participants in the collective project of sustainability. The leverage of moral authority is in how it recruits the identity and emotional commitment of the believer into the new paradigm. By emphasizing how humanity is *totally dependent on* nature's health for our existence and survival, we invoke the metaphorical and conceptual grounding of moral ladders and hierarchies along with the new conceptual ideas of the ecological worldview.

Initiation into any belief system begins as people learn to "see through the lens" of a perspective by being shown or taught how to do it. As discussed earlier, new knowledge—which challenges the mind to take another perspective—is the most direct and likely way to shake a person loose from an existing paradigm. In the case of ecology, it might come from watching a movie, walking through a forest with a naturalist guide, having an inspiring conversation with someone studying ecology, or even from reading an emotionally involving article or book. *An alternative to the conventional mindset will appeal to people if and only if they begin to think about humanity and the biosphere from an ecological perspective.*

Bringing an ecological perspective to nature and humanity is a learning experience proceeding at a different pace for each person. Somewhere along this journey, the interdependence of our species and its environment will come into focus. Once someone comes to understand that we all depend on the health of the biosphere for survival, *internalizing* the value of this relationship, granting legitimate authority to nature will just feel like the right thing to do.[5]

The framing of paradigms and belief systems never occurs in a vacuum. What I am advocating here is a particular construction of the ecological worldview that takes into account this moment in history, of a global crisis not only of climate change but also of political, economic, and cultural inertia. Specifically, as the previous chapter explained, the best scientific understanding of our relationship to nature is one of *interdependence*, more like reciprocity and partnership, not one of dominance. Human *dependence* on nature has no intrinsic priority in an ecological worldview; however, it is the factor with the greatest motivational force for human survival, which is why it should be front and center in any discussion of the ecological crisis.

The answer to the question posed in this chapter—How *should* we construe the relationship of humankind to the Earth's biosphere?—is that humanity is *totally dependent on* nature's health for our existence and survival. The reason to construe it this way is that it captures the essential lesson that we should/must bend our wills to restoring the health of nature to secure our survival. It is also the reason we should willingly grant moral authority to "life's healthy operating principles" to serve as ethical guidelines for humanity. The following chapter is devoted to examining what those principles might be.

7
LIFE'S HEALTHY OPERATING PRINCIPLES

*Once we see nature as a mentor, our relationship with the
living world changes.*

— Janine M. Benyus (1997)[1]

Sustainability

This chapter draws on the preceding ones to identify the patterns
and principles that account for the biosphere's sustainability.
How does nature keep itself healthy indefinitely? To set the
context, let's begin by revisiting our working premises and
clarifying what "healthy" means.

We presume that humanity is an interconnected *part* of
nature, *totally dependent on* nature's health for our existence
and survival; that entrenched, intensive, worldwide industrial
development is severely damaging the biosphere's health on
an ongoing basis, directly threatening human survival; and
that humankind isn't currently able to take the threat seriously
enough to save ourselves before it is too late. It follows from
these premises that any prescription for human survival must
include a plan to restore and maintain biosphere health.

In this context, "healthy" is to be understood holistically. A healthy living system is not only free from disease and infirmity, but also optimizes its bonds and relationships with other members of its ecological community for the mutual benefit of all. This broad, systemic conception of healthy subsumes the notion of "well-being." Healthy plants and animals exude vital energy. A healthier human being will be more productive, live longer, and experience more happiness and fulfillment. An optimum state of health is a fully realized phenotype of its genotype, a perfect expression of being alive.

For all ecosystems, being healthy also means persisting over long periods of time and across unpredictably varied conditions; in other words, being *sustainably* healthy. Sustainability is a much greater achievement than mere viability in the here and now. It entails such accomplishments as the recycling of renewable energy, the ability to self-regulate and self-renew, and a robust capacity to adapt to new challenges, as well as mechanisms of succession of species when environmental conditions undergo radical change.

At this critical moment, humanity must reinvent itself to live healthfully and sustainably, so that our civilization can fit into the biosphere as a cooperating partner in the great web of life, not as the destructive and self-destructive force we are at present. Understanding the biosphere's operating patterns and principles is a necessary first step in understanding what we must do next.

Systems Dynamics and Operational Principles, Interwoven

Seeing nature through an ecological lens reveals a magnificent array of patterns and themes. The phenomena essential to healthy and sustainable ecosystems have different qualities in different combinations, so no flat list of items or simple categories can do them justice. The patterns that stand out are ubiquitous *systems dynamics*, the patterns of functional relationships that recur at different levels of organization throughout nature. The themes appear as common *operational principles and strategies*. In reality, these patterns and themes frequently interweave and overlap, as will be apparent in the descriptions that follow.

First and foremost among system dynamics is **interdependence**. Life presents itself to us as a pattern of relationships among entities interconnected in a vast network of feedback loops, which create multiple levels of dependencies among the entities. The network pattern of organization creates reciprocal, mutual dependencies between the parts and the whole. Our own bodies exemplify this. Your body needs your heart and lungs to perform vital functions continuously. Your heart and lungs in turn depend on a vascular system and smooth muscles to do their respective jobs. Your brain keeps track of what's going on everywhere in your body. All the while, it's equally true that your heart, lungs, blood vessels, and muscles must exist in the context of your body to perform their designated functions. The entire ensemble of cells and organs of the human body operates as a coherent whole precisely because of the intricate interdependencies within the ensemble.

Among social animals—especially humans—the same kinds of interdependencies exist in social relations as a result of intentional acts of cooperation, reciprocity, and partnership. The pattern of multiple feedback loops in social networks is functionally identical to that of biological interdependence. But **cooperation** (without conscious intent) is worth calling out separately from interdependencies in general to highlight its special importance in nonhuman nature. The recombination of genes, symbiosis among tiny creatures, and other types of cooperative synergies have been primary means of generating novelty in natural selection.[2] Cooperation succeeds in natural selection because it increases fitness across the widest range of niches. Despite contrary claims from ideological proponents of competition, cooperation is the primary interrelationship among entities at all levels of the biosphere, including any sustainable human civilization.

In nature, all **parts act to secure the whole, under the whole's direction**. Within an all-encompassing network architecture, living systems and subsystems are nested inside each other in hierarchies of size and hierarchies of control. Structural hierarchies are typically visible as smaller and larger sized entities (like "Russian dolls"), while control hierarchies, comprising multiple feedback loops, bear no necessary relationship to visible structures. Control hierarchies are the means by which nature achieves exquisite coordination of parts and wholes at multiple levels of complex living systems. Described earlier as "downward causation," the top level of a system passes reference values as inputs to its parts at lower levels, thereby controlling their actions. In broad strokes, this is how Earth's biosphere achieves the coordination of its subordinate ecosystems.

Living systems and their environments are interactively coupled through boundaries into integrated wholes. They are so tightly coupled as to be essentially one unit. Every cell is bounded by a membrane that constitutes the boundary between its inner and outer environments; without a boundary there is no such entity as a cell. At the same time, each cell is selectively "open" to its outer environment, meaning that sources of energy or information can flow into and out of the system through its boundary, as allowed by the cell membrane. Outside nutrients and energy are required for metabolism, the cell's network of chemical reactions that sustain life. No living thing, from single-celled bacteria to entire ecosystems, can exist without an appropriate environment.

Another fundamental system dynamic in nature is *cyclical processes* (cycles), which include day and night, high and low tides, and seasons of the year; as well as metabolism (Fig. 5.1, chapter five), and the photosynthesis-driven food cycle (Fig. 5.2, chapter five). The first three cycles result from Earth's relations to other extraterrestrial objects and its movements in space. They have been constant and essential features of the environment within which all life evolved, which means that everything alive today evolved in one way or another to fit into and take advantage of these cycles. The latter two cycles are the means by which organisms derive the energy they need to survive. The **circular causation** pattern (Fig 4.1, chapter four) common to all five cycles is the dynamic of all the feedback control systems that collectively enable the biosphere to self-regulate.

Sunlight provides the energy that runs virtually all life on Earth.[3] Photosynthesis in green plants converts solar energy into chemical energy bound into organic substances. In the food cycle (Fig. 5.2, chapter 5), communities of organisms reuse the same molecules of minerals, water, and air; and waste from one species provides food for another. In this manner, **nature recycles everything**. Recycling is the prime example of nature's highly efficient use of energy.[4]

All living systems rely on **self-regulation** to operate within **critical limits**. To survive even as environmental conditions fluctuate, every organism requires an internal milieu of chemical and thermal parameters maintained within rather narrow tolerance ranges, or critical limits. **Homeostasis** is the self-regulation control system built into every organism to maintain vital parameters within their critical limits. Ecosystems have an added critical limit to consider: the population of one species or another the particular environment can sustain. This limit is called its **carrying capacity**. Ecosystems continue to self-regulate as a population threatens to exceed its carrying capacity, but exceeding its limit causes a breakdown.

The Earth's biosphere has been successfully self-regulating the chemical composition of the atmosphere (the percentages of and balance between oxygen and carbon dioxide) to keep Earth's surface temperature hospitable to life for billions of years. Human disruption of this process is the crux of the climate crisis and the proximate reason we must reinvent ourselves if our species is to survive.

All living systems have **internal mechanisms to correct disturbances** from the limits and interdependencies of the system as a whole. Homeostasis is the fundamental and first line of defense by maintaining vital parameters within critical range. Newly created somatic cells with defects are automatically rejected by the processes monitoring growth and replacement of cells; one result is that most cancerous cells are rejected before they can do global damage. Static immune systems expand this protective capability to microbial pathogens. Adaptive immune systems learn by exposure how to prevent repeated incursions of harmful bacteria and viruses. And during early stages of development, most embryos or fetuses with critical abnormalities are naturally aborted. These are among the internal survival mechanisms of organisms. Ecosystems have survival mechanisms of their own. For example, when a forest burns down, buried seeds remain to provide for restoration as conditions permit.

Nature uses limits and constraints to its advantage. Boundaries create limits in space which constrain both the internal and external environments of any living system; neither metabolism nor self-regulation could occur without boundaries. Homeostasis uses critical tolerance limits to regulate parameters of chemicals in the organism's internal milieu. The laws of physics and energy efficiency constrain organisms from growing too large for their energy supply systems; these limits are coded into genetic instructions that regulate somatic cell division appropriately.

Nature balances stability with flexibility. Even one-celled organisms combine core survival processes, which are mainly focused on maintaining optimal internal conditions, with more open-ended, flexible adaptive mechanisms. This combination of stability with at least some flexibility is found everywhere in the biosphere. Up the evolutionary ladder, more complex and sensitive adaptive capabilities extend the scope of external conditions organisms can accommodate. The human brain is the ultimate example of advanced adaptive capacities, including open-ended languages, limitless mental maps and models of the physical, social, and symbolic worlds in which we live, and learning to keep learning as circumstances change. *To be alive is always to be adapting to changing circumstances.*

Nature's ultimate adaptive process is biological evolution, which capitalizes on variation within populations of organisms. The fitness criteria of changing, unpredictable circumstances drives natural selection toward organisms with greater and greater adaptive capacities. Within populations, **evolution also trends toward increased diversity**. Nature benefits when the pruning function of natural selection is applied to a diverse rather than a limited set of options. Ecosystems evolve to be adapted to particular, local, physical environments, exemplifying the *specificity* of adaptation, which results in more diversity, both within and between ecosystems. Diversity ensures a robust capacity to survive unpredictable changes, a winning sustainability strategy. Some seedlings survive a forest fire better than others. Some humans have a natural resistance to diseases that others don't.

Taken together, the preceding suite of patterns, principles, and strategies accounts for the sustainability of the biosphere, the great achievement of biological evolution that humanity must now learn how to achieve for itself. In chapter nine, I derive a set of "lessons for sustainability" from the patterns and principles identified in this chapter. These lessons are how I map life's healthy operating principles into the space of opportunities for human civilization to live and function more sustainably

Humanity's Dependency on Biosphere Health

Humanity's dependency on the biosphere's health—and the consequences of fouling our own nest—can be boiled down to a few main points:

- Humans can survive only when our *internal* environmental conditions remain within critical tolerance levels. Our homeostatic systems provide leeway as external temperatures or dietary regimens fluctuate, but humans die rather quickly under extremes of temperature or without oxygen to breathe, and within days without water to drink. Thus, human survival depends on our *external* environment continuing to provide conditions befitting our critical tolerance levels.

- Individually and collectively, humans are interactively coupled to our external environment, both in the moment (breathing, drinking, eating) and over time. Our survival is increasingly threatened by human pollution of our own surroundings, which poisons air, water, and food, as well as by such global climate events as extreme temperatures, winds, floods, and pandemics. Because we are so tightly coupled with our external environment, we can't escape dependence on the biosphere's health.

- Pumping and dumping industrial waste products into the atmosphere and biosphere has already exceeded their carrying capacities for these materials, seriously disrupting nature's own recycling and self-regulation processes. Humanity may survive the short-term (decades) consequences of this disruption, albeit with increasing loss of life and widespread suffering, but before too long the biosphere's self-regulation systems will break down. No one can predict the precise consequences of this breakdown, but the survival of our species is not likely to be one of them.

Let us review and take stock of where humanity stands in relation to the wisdom of nature laid out in this chapter. Our entire culturally-entrenched industrial civilization is built on an economic growth paradigm and supporting beliefs that were once emancipating but have become self-destructive. If our goal is, as it must be, to achieve global sustainability compatible with human health and survival, we must recognize that we are falling farther and farther behind each day despite the heroic efforts of millions of climate activists and like-minded citizens around the world. An increasing minority of progressive businesses are investing in sustainable practices, which serve as examples and inspiration to the rest of us. But a critical mass of humanity does not understand the nature of the climate crisis or the urgency of dramatic action. As discussed in the previous chapter, it's not that planet Earth needs saving, it's that humanity is at risk of self-extinction![5]

Major Issues for Humanity

The remainder of this book advocates a post-industrial worldview grounded in naturalist and humanist ethics. As a transition to that focus, let us preview some major issues for humanity raised by the patterns and principles discussed in this chapter. From a bird's-eye view, I see three dimensions along which industrial civilization is fundamentally at odds with sustainability.

Time Scale – Nature has been playing a "long game" (of sustainability) for billions of years. In particular, nature recycles renewable resources and aborts destructive processes from within. Human civilization has been operating in direct opposition to these practices for the last few centuries. This opposition is not a mere matter of tweaking how we play the game. Humans are notoriously unable to trade off long-term payoffs for short-term gains (unless laws or regulations force us to behave differently). We are voracious and indiscriminate consumers of resources (unless governments impose strict penalties for specific behaviors). And we predictably wait until innovations demonstrate intolerable consequences before we stop to think whether it was a good idea to adopt them in the first place.

Our civilization's relationship with time is critically out of whack. In particular, we must find a way to greatly slow down our ("24/7") obscenely short financial transaction and news cycles, while at the same time figuring out how to dramatically speed up our entire economy's transformation to renewable energy. Beyond that, humans can reinvent themselves to live sustainably by adopting values that derive from nature's healthy operating principles.

Unconstrained Growth – Nature regulates itself relentlessly, thereby optimizing its network of cyclical, systemic interrelationships, and preventing unconstrained positive feedback processes from disrupting the dynamic balance of whole organisms or ecosystems. Meanwhile, capitalism, our dominant economic system, measures success as a function of growth in either "gross domestic product" (nations) or profits (companies), both of which are expected to grow at least linearly or, even better, exponentially for an indefinite time.

Markets are unforgiving of companies whose rate of growth tapers off. Capitalists in America reflexively reject regulation as a constraint on economic growth; however, without extensive regulation, it's impossible to reconcile the opposite growth dynamics of nature and capitalism. Like Father Time, Mother Nature is inescapable: only extensive, constraining regulation can save capitalism from self-destruction. We must adopt different values, different goals, and different measures of economic success in the nearest achievable future.

Domination – Domination in nature is the exception rather than the rule. It occurs most commonly when animals compete for mating partners or for scarce food or water supplies, and less commonly to establish a pecking order among social animals. These behaviors are significant, to be sure, but we mentally inflate their prevalence because they are so often the focus of nature documentaries, which thrive on the ideological and dramatic power of competition. Otherwise, for all other purposes, partnership, cooperation, and coordination are the most common relationships in interdependent networks of organisms and ecosystems throughout the biosphere. Humanity, in contrast, has a long history of slavery, colonialism, and patriarchy, as well as wars fought over territory or between groups claiming superiority over other groups. These examples of conquest or domination by force reflect the same primal urge, to feel superior to others by treating them as inferior.

However, there is another, equally fundamental, primal urge of *homo sapiens*: to connect, coordinate, and cooperate with each other to achieve common goals, as demonstrated by humanity's long history of productive accomplishments. What always brings people together is common interests. And when it comes to the biosphere and sustainability, humans have the most overriding possible common interest in our survival as a species. We don't all have to love each other to work together effectively for a common goal. But it does help immeasurably to live in a society providing opportunities for recognition and fulfillment without the need to belittle others. Naturalist and humanist values offer the most direct means to attain such a society.

The American version of hyper-individualism is also on a collision course with any program to achieve sustainability. Like all other living systems, human individuals are intrinsically autonomous, goal-directed, and adaptive. But how individuals relate to others, and to the whole of society, varies greatly from one culture to another. The differences between an "independent" self and an "interdependent" self were discussed in chapter one. For individuals who see themselves as interdependent with others, the leap to being interdependent with the biosphere is far less daunting than for individuals whose self is intrinsically independent of others. Along this dimension, American individualism is an outlier, even within the relatively individualistic bent of Western societies.[6]

Because humanity is an interconnected *part* of nature, *totally dependent on* nature's health for our existence and survival, the patterns, principles, and strategies of a healthy biosphere must become *moral guideposts* for us. Sustainability is the ultimate goal of living systems, and the means by which nature achieves sustainability are effectively nature's purposes, goals, or "values." If humans are to achieve sustainability, we must incorporate these values into our lives. In fact, if we are to achieve sustainability soon enough to avert our own extinction, we must elevate these values to our highest priorities. In the following chapters, I will spell out what it would mean for humanity to adopt a natural humanist worldview, a worldview in harmony with nature's healthy operating principles.

PART III

NATURAL HUMANISM

What we lack... is the social guidance system, the governing values, that would redirect the allocation of resources, including our advanced technological knowhow, to higher ends.

— **Riane Eisler (1988)**[1]

Part III marks this book's transition from the domain of *is* to the domain of *ought*. Parts I and II presented descriptive and explanatory essays about humanity's interrelationships with culture and with the biosphere, emphasizing differences between present and former ways of thinking. Occasional glimpses of natural humanism's worldview foreshadowed the full portrayal, offered here, in the five chapters constituting Part III.

The first chapter, "Naturalist Morality," provides the rationale for normative principles grounded in nature and a naturalist interpretation of human needs, instead of the more traditional supernatural or transcendental sources of authority. The second chapter, "Life's Lessons for Sustainability," draws lessons from nature about how living systems function successfully, and spells out the critical values, goals, and strategies that will allow humanity to survive the climate crisis by achieving a sustainable way of life. The third chapter, "Humanist Values and Principles," describes in greater detail the premises and implications of a philosophy that prioritizes social justice, subordinating capitalist priorities to the health, well-being, and fulfillment of all human beings.

The fourth chapter, "Toward a Natural Humanist Society," considers what changes we might expect to see in society if there were to be a meaningful shift in belief from the established neoliberal worldview toward natural humanism. The fifth chapter, "Summary and Implications," highlights the key elements of divergence between neoliberalism and natural humanism, and the three main tenets of natural humanism and their implications.

––––––––––––

As previously spelled out in the book's Introduction, natural humanism rests on two fundamental premises: naturalism and social constructionism. Naturalism is logically prior to social constructionism because its first axiom is that the "natural" world is the only world that exists. The concept of a supernatural or transcendent source of truth or virtue is a fictional creation of human imagination. Humanity is made entirely of nature. We (our bodies, cultures, economies, and beliefs) are enmeshed in the natural world, continuously interacting with nature on a hierarchy of levels from individual metabolism through our whole species and the whole biosphere. Given this premise, the only possible grounding for moral philosophy is to be found in nature and a naturalist interpretation of human needs.

Social constructionism is best understood in the context of the human condition, our unique niche in nature, humans being both fully animal and distinctively mindful. Like all animals, our biological propensities are predetermined by evolutionary history. And, like all higher primates, humans are biologically prepared for active social, emotional, and mental lives. However, as discussed in detail in Part I, our unique, definitive biological heritage is our capacity for open-ended symbolic representation, with which humans collectively *construct our own social reality* in the medium of *culture.*

Humans construct social reality (language, traditions, norms, institutions) through continuing interactions with their local, national, and global cultures. All knowledge is understood from some *perspective*; there is no such thing as pure, transcendent, perfectly objective knowledge. There are no facts without some frame or theory within which to identify them. All frames, theories, and similar conceptual filters manifest the knower's perspective. Because *actual reality* is so vast and complex—far beyond comprehension from any one perspective—there is no such thing as a best or universal perspective; all viewpoints are intrinsically limited and incomplete.

Given these premises, the proper grounds for valid (socially agreed-upon) knowledge are an inclusive and participatory democracy, a privileged role for the skeptical empiricism of science, and an insistence on diversity and pluralism—all cultural practices that embody or embrace multiple perspectives. As Part III will demonstrate, if the essential fabric and first principles of culture consist of genuine democracy, a proper role for science, and the full embrace of diversity and pluralism, those practices in tandem will function as society's "immune system," securing it against self-induced social disruption, just as a biological immune system works dynamically to protect its body from both internal and external threats.

8
NATURALIST MORALITY[1]

A naturalist morality is different in principle from the historically dominant moral systems of philosophical and religious traditions that emphasize universal moral absolutes emanating from ultimate principles or transcendent authorities. Whether religious or secular, conventional moral systems presume a timeless universality of moral rules and principles that by one means or another originate outside the culture of which they are actually a part. Although circumstances are paid due respect in interpretation and application, traditional morality is assumed to have a *given* truth to it, an inevitability originating either with God or as universal *a priori* principles. By contrast, a naturalist morality is intrinsically pragmatic and fallible, a human social construction built on the foundation of our biological predispositions.

Morality is about a community's normative issues: what we consider to be good or bad, and right or wrong. What are our bedrock values? The ultimate normative issue is which authority decides the answers to normative questions. Who gets to tell the stories that legitimate what's right and wrong? As discussed in Part I, the answer depends on which worldview is operative because each worldview specifies its own version of knowledge, values, and ultimate source of authority. Religious worldviews generally invoke a higher, timeless, and transcendental authority; atheists rely on empiricism and rationality; and naturalists take their cues from Mother Nature. Worldviews are not mutually exclusive; in particular, empiricism is a foundational principle for atheists and naturalists alike. But each worldview has its own "internal logic," emphasizing its own focal issues, arguments, and justifications, and encompassing its own system of morality.

Natural humanism is grounded in explicit premises: naturalism, constructionism (in culture), the human condition, existential dilemmas, and pluralism. These premises are what most clearly delineate the differences between natural humanism and other worldviews. A naturalist morality does not generally prescribe or proscribe specific behaviors or rules. It is a subject for reflection and deliberation from multiple perspectives. My main focus is on values, goals, principles, and normative strategies at a level of generality suited to local adaptation and culturally-specific interpretation.

In pluralist societies, adherents of different worldviews typically co-exist and are obliged if not required to negotiate with each other in political arenas. However, the unprecedented, uniquely *global* threat of the climate crisis urgently demands *global* resolutions to numerous normative issues with huge economic consequences. Unfortunately, humanity has been stuck for decades on how to arrive at, legitimate, and enforce effective sustainability resolutions at a global level. We confronted this challenge in chapter six and will revisit it in chapter nine. Meanwhile, this chapter is devoted to what naturalist morality means within the worldview of natural humanism.

My rationale for a naturalist morality begins with the foundational premise of pluralism: Because *actual reality* is so vast and complex—far beyond comprehension from any one perspective—there can be no such thing as one best or universal perspective; *all* points of view are intrinsically limited and incomplete. Every meaningful question implicates some framing to establish context and is necessarily subject to more than one interpretation. Accordingly, only processes encompassing a diversity of views can reasonably hope to achieve legitimacy in any contested moral or political domain.

Pluralism is not only a compelling philosophical premise, but also a necessary practical stance in today's postmodern world because multiple worldviews are always in play, often within families and classrooms as well as at national and global levels. Moreover, in chapter three, we concluded that humans effectively live within their own, self-constructed belief systems, each one providing its own version of the truth. Thus, in our contemporary pluralistic world, universal moral absolutes from transcendent authorities no longer make sense. The appropriate alternative to a transcendent or supernatural authority is to look to the natural world—*our species-wide collective home*—as the fount of values and guides to action. What does morality amount to when we rely solely on what we can learn from the study of nature and human experience?

Biological Roots

Recall our premise about the human condition: To be human is to be both fully animal and distinctively mindful at the same time, with all the challenges and complexities this duality entails. As social animals, humans inherit the same basic nervous system and emotional proclivities as our closest evolutionary cousins and fellow social animals, chimpanzees and bonobos. These biological propensities are a significant part of the human genetic endowment and are never far from consideration when mindful humans collectively construct moral systems. Naturalist morality rests on a foundation of these biological roots, which reside in the suite of emotionally-driven social behaviors that humans share with chimps and bonobos.[2]

From the perspective of neuroscience, these common emotional responses reflect similar subcortical brain structures, and the unconscious control of emotion by neurotransmitters and hormones such as dopamine, serotonin, oxytocin, and endorphins. Chimps, bonobos, and humans respond similarly to socially relevant triggers under genetic control, guided by the neural release of pleasure and pain chemicals, which function as anticipatory signals as well as rewards and punishments.[3]

The fundamental prosocial emotion is empathy, which is rooted in the instinctive bond between mother and child, the archetype of social relations. All social animals respond empathetically to signs of others' distress, and more generally care about the well-being of others in their group. Scientists recently discovered a class of cells in animal brains that respond equally when we perform an action and when we witness someone else perform the same action. These so-called "mirror" neurons most likely underlie not only all the many forms that empathy can take but also such notable prosocial instincts as mimicry and social contagion.

Social animals evolved because groups have survival advantages over individuals. The survival value of group life manifests itself in the mental and emotional life of chimps and bonobos as a consistent bias toward prosocial behavior. From our common ancestors, apes and humans also inherit a propensity to divide the world into "us" and "them," reserving warm and fuzzy feelings for those we identify as insiders and harboring antisocial tendencies toward outsiders. Another important aspect of our inherited concern for harmonious social life is everyone's sensitivity to status, rank, and hierarchy. When group equilibrium is upset, individuals act appropriately to make amends and rectify the disruption. Cooperation and a strong sense of fairness plausibly evolved from needing to maintain harmony in the face of resource competition while hunting and sharing meat in groups.[4]

To succeed as group members, we social animals require not only some conception of how things are supposed to be (an image of what's right and what's wrong), but also the cognitive ability to control impulses and inhibit inappropriate behaviors. Young apes and humans may inherit prosocial tendencies, but they still have to learn how *not* to act *in*appropriately. To this end, as children get older, selective punishment is effective in achieving internalization of prosocial habits. Frans de Waal aptly sums up these dynamics:

> *Two great reinforcers support the social code by which primates and children live. One comes from within and one comes from without. The first is empathy and a desire for good relations leading to the avoidance of unnecessary distress. The second is the threat of physical consequences, such as penalties meted out by higher-ups. Over time, these two reinforcers create an internalized set of guidelines.*[5]

To be clear, I take the social-emotional continuities between apes and young children as strong evidence for the biological *roots* of human morality; but the prosocial behavior of chimps and bonobos in itself does not constitute morality as humans understand it. We do have similar emotional dynamics, but apes are lacking the distinctly human characteristics of shared intentionality and a collective conception of morality. Unlike our nearest primate relatives, we think abstractly about moral principles, rules of conduct, and the welfare of the community as a whole, including people we will never meet. What deserves emphasis is that the biological roots of morality are species-wide: all humans are social animals, and thereby inheritors of the same basic emotional make-up as chimps and bonobos. These are facts that any moral system should take into account.

Equally worthy of emphasis is that biology is not destiny. Inheritance guides but does not dictate behavior. Innate tendencies, inclinations, and propensities are at most default initial conditions. Our ultimate behavior is caused by the cumulative combined effects of inheritance, parenting, peers, education, other life experiences, and the norms, habits, and belief systems particular to the culture(s) and era in which we grow up. As one example, some aggressive men will tend to use physical force to get their way; some will play contact sports; some will do battle with fellow academics, business competitors, or ideological opponents; and some will join the military and perhaps go to war. Others may be satisfied with video games, heavy metal guitar, or some other totally symbolic outlet for their aggressive tendencies. The permutations are endless.

Existential Dilemmas

Beyond the biological, species-wide roots of morality, humans have always debated normative issues with great intensity. It may be an overreach to suggest that belief systems evolved *in order to* rationalize and legitimate moral principles, but doing so is undoubtedly one of their primary practical functions. On the one hand each worldview encompasses its own system of morality. On the other hand, due to humanity's shared evolutionary history, all worldviews face the same fundamental normative challenges or "existential dilemmas." Any list of existential dilemmas is necessarily incomplete and suggestive, but the following three belong on any short list of essential issues for any moral system: Us versus Them, Domination versus Partnership, and Self-Interest versus Community Concern. Needless to say, these issues intertwine. The following brief discussion of these issues illustrates the spirit and general approach of a naturalist morality.

Us versus Them

Humans inherit a tendency to act prosocially toward members of their own group and antisocially toward members of other groups. The "other" may be based on appearance (skin color), territory (nationality), familiarity (status or class), beliefs (religious or political ideology), or something totally arbitrary. Of relatively minor import, sports teams that compete regularly often develop some animosity toward their opponents; and their fans tend to mimic these attitudes. Of major import, racist and ideological hatred are two of the most powerful forces driving political unrest and authoritarian leadership across the globe.

I do not imagine that innate tendencies to categorize people by group, and to like some people more than others, will ever disappear; nor will the emotional "ties that bind" us to our families, childhood friends, and tribes. But I do believe that harm from antisocial behavior toward others can be greatly diminished, and that our prosocial feelings for "people like me" are susceptible to major expansion through education and life experiences that change the meaning and increase the scope of the "people like me" category.[6]

The single most potent method of bringing people together is to meet their basic human needs for food, shelter, health care, education, and a meaningful role in society through work or other service. People get along with each other much better when they are not deprived, anxious, or fearful, and when they are not competing for essential resources as a result of real or artificially created scarcities. *Care and nurturance* are not only intrinsically satisfying moral practices but also policies that preemptively minimize the costs societies otherwise would bear from preventable mental and physical illness, drug abuse, violent crime, and other "social" pathologies.

In addition, the policies and practices of identifying and focusing on common interests, common goals, and *the common good*[7] make all the usual differences among groups less salient, less important, and less harmful. A transparent and accountable political regime of *democracy* (self-determination) *and humanist values* would build solidarity and go a long way toward effectively neutralizing the politics of division and demagoguery.

Globalization and the Internet have made us all more familiar with others' cultures than we used to be. A normative paradigm shift toward *pluralism and diversity* would change the meaning and scope of "people like me," recasting the idea of "otherness" from an inherent negative to a presumptive benefit. If one believes there is only one right answer (ours), multiple points of view (theirs) are disruptive and detrimental. If diversity were recognized as the linchpin of a society's strength and resilience, as it should be, "others" would be welcomed inside the tent, not kept out of it.

When demagogic leaders successfully exploit latent emotions to pit groups against each other, our first instinct is to attribute their success to human vulnerability, rather than to the social and economic conditions that provided fertile ground for exploitation. But demagogues succeed in turning people against each other only when times are hard and people are predisposed to scapegoat. The great danger in this political dynamic is the amplifying feedback loop that feeds a demagogue's strength. When a leader like Donald Trump rips apart the normative fabric of a society to secure his own power, it is the destruction and absence of the usual social constraints that unleashes antisocial mob behavior. The best way to avoid the rise of demagogic leaders is to provide sufficient social and economic benefits to inoculate the public against them.

Finally, and pertinent to how the three existential dilemmas interrelate: I believe the problems inherent in the "us versus them" dilemma would be significantly diminished to the extent that societies tilt (a) toward egalitarian partnership and away from domination hierarchies; and (b) toward community concern and away from self-interest. A naturalist morality resolves these dichotomies on the side of humanism.

Domination versus Partnership

Animals compete with each other as necessary for limited resources such as territory, mating partners, food, and water. Social animals also jockey for status and rank. Even young children intuitively sort themselves into a "pecking" order, with those of higher rank enjoying privileged attention, leading or bossing others around, and enforcing group norms. Youngsters like to confront their elders in competitive tests of status and rank. It is not unusual for winners and losers of status contests to react emotionally with displays of dominance (chest thumping) or submission (slouching). This localized kind of dominance and acting out is a common feature of competitions within families (sibling rivalries), social groups, leagues, associations, and communities of practice (the quadrennial Olympics).

Whether formal or informal, seeking status or a conference trophy, competitive dominance plays a valued and legitimate role in existing social structures. Its legitimacy rests on the fact that individuals of lower status or rank not only aspire to higher status or rank but also *willingly* accept their position in the scheme of things. Perceived fairness is essential to legitimacy; everybody must play by the same rules. What matters is that winners and losers alike accept and *internalize* the validity of the whole system, be it their social community, a sports league, or a national election. Domination as the outcome of fair competition is an accepted part of life for social animals. It is part of our biological heritage.

There are countless other social contexts in which status and rank determine relationships. A major subset are hierarchical relationships, in which higher ranks give directives to lower ranks which (must) follow them. This "chain of command" is most explicit in the military, but the same basic logic applies to bureaucracies in most organizations, profit or nonprofit, private or public sector. Still, organizations vary greatly in how they are managed, from dominator hierarchies in the military and related industries to partnerships characteristic of creative groups in the arts and entertainment worlds. In dominator hierarchies, power and control flow in one direction, from top to bottom. By default, the authority in a dominator hierarchy is obeyed but not necessarily perceived as legitimate; well-managed organizations support subordinates well enough to earn their trust. In partnerships, control flows back and forth, each partner providing both benefits and constraints for the other(s). Partnerships are a reciprocity-based form of cooperation, true cases of legitimate authority as long as partners are on the same wavelength.[8]

In sharp contrast, consider humanity's long history and continued attachment to domination maintained by brute force or the threat of it, a morally repugnant[9] extrapolation from dominator hierarchies with no precedent in non-human nature—a human cultural invention completely devoid of fairness or legitimacy. Instances as different as slavery, patriarchy, and colonial empires are linked by the common pattern of three elements: (a) assertion of absolute authority to dominate, (b) use of actual or threatened harm to enforce it, and (c) some story about a *natural moral order* serving to justify the assertion of domination and its punitive enforcement.

The core justification for absolute authority is belief in the *inherent superiority* of one group over another; in the case of domination by force (and terrorism), the relevant "superior" groups are Whites over Blacks (racism), Men over Women (misogyny), and Believers over Infidels (apostasy). The belief in superiority warrants a license to humiliate and exploit the inferior party. In extreme cases it becomes a mandate to dehumanize and treat them as property, even to murder them. The perpetrators are almost always male. (But research does not support a simple association between aggression and testosterone.)[10]

Domination by force is clearly related to antagonism between "us" and "them." One common thread is the inherited tendency to categorize by groups. Another commonality is the very wide range of feelings and behaviors between inherited tendencies and social outcomes. Consider the vast difference between an inherited preference for hanging out with "people like me" and a belief in white supremacy; or between feeling discomfort around unfamiliar people and feeling hatred toward all people of a certain kind. The beliefs that fuel these differences are cultural, not biological; socially constructed, not genetically determined. They are passed on from one generation to another by parents and peer groups, and reinforced by like-minded social support systems.[11] Belief systems embracing a "natural" order of *inherent* superiority of one category of people over another category of people are abhorrent. If humanity is to get its act together in time to save ourselves from climate catastrophe, these belief systems need to be eviscerated and overridden by humanistic social movements with a great sense of urgency!

What can replace the belief of so many people in a natural order justifying their own superiority? Nothing short of a new worldview to replace the old. The alternative vision—the compound strategy—is for culture to provide a multitude of ways for people to receive recognition, affirmation, status, and fulfillment that don't depend on putting other people down, in tandem with the strategies offered above for mitigating the us-them dilemma: a democratic society that meets basic human needs, focuses on the common good, and embraces pluralism and diversity. To complete the picture, top it off with empathetic classroom teachers and parents who use contingent nurturance rather than absolute dominance to control their children.

Self-Interest versus Community Concern

No group of any size can function effectively as a collective entity without a way to suppress disruptive self-serving behavior.[12] Teachers must keep disruptive students in line for the benefit of the whole class. Societies must enforce sanctions against those who pollute the community's fresh air and clean water. The culture in some societies produces individuals whose concern for community is greater than their own self-interest. Recall from chapter one that in Japanese and other Eastern cultures, one's self is understood to be *interdependent* with others, unlike America and other Western cultures where the self is constructed to be *independent* of others. More generally, Eastern cultures tend to be more collectivist than individualist; Western cultures tend to be more individualist than collectivist.

There is nothing intrinsically wrong with individualism, nor is individualism necessarily at odds with community concern. I can imagine an ideal society carved so as to balance individual needs with community needs, perhaps even to the degree that the two support each other.[13] What is morally problematic is the presumption of *self-interest* built into capitalism. Over the years, capitalism's dominant role in American culture has threatened to overshadow or even override other values. A trend toward significant counterbalancing norms, laws, and values began in the 1930s with New Deal commitments to the public good such as labor laws, public works, safety net payments, and incentives and subsidies for public education. The common good continued to be supported after World War II through the G.I. Bill, the national highway system, national parks, civil rights and voting rights legislation, and federal funding for Health, Education, and Welfare. Due to the longtime influence of economist John Maynard Keynes, a political consensus resulted in a decades-long period of sustained economic growth under a *managed* market economy.

Since 1980, however, a dominant neoliberal (free-market) political regime has embraced rampant self-interest at the expense of community concern, willfully aiming to suffocate the public sector while dismantling labor unions and the collective protections they provided. In brief, the regime focused on (a) maximizing profits and minimizing taxes for corporate share-holders, global corporations, and wealthy individuals, thereby depriving the community of financial resources to meet public needs; (b) minimizing corporate liability for damage to public goods and resources, thereby disabling the community from protecting its own interests; and (c) using wealth (funding elections and lobbying congress) and disinformation (Fox News et al.) to preserve political dominance, undermine public trust, and disenfranchise voters. In addition, government institutions have been attacked persistently as incompetent and untrustworthy, and hence not a source of collective solutions to social and economic problems—in stark contrast to the New Deal era, when millions looked to the federal government in the face of the collapse of the private sector economy.

The consequences of neoliberalism for many Americans have been disastrous. A short list includes replacement of most middle-class manufacturing jobs with low-income service jobs; growth of a frightening culture of guns, violence, and militarized police officers; and three broad realms of decimation: health care, economic inequality, and environmental degradation. The U.S. health care system is by far the most expensive in the world, yet we have the lowest life expectancy and highest suicide rate among high-income nations.[14] The most striking development in the U.S. economy over the last four decades is the stagnation of incomes of the bottom 50% relative to the upsurge in incomes of the top 1%. Measured in constant 2016 dollars, average pre-tax income for the bottom 50% has stagnated at around $16,500 since 1980, while the top 1% has experienced 300% growth in income to approximately $1,340,000 in 2014![15] Meanwhile, our window of opportunity to manage global warming is rapidly disappearing, leaving the entire planet in a state of climate crisis.

American individualism has never been more extreme. Not too long ago, we were a country of citizens, most of whom studied civics in public school. Now we are all consumers, subject to a constant onslaught of targeted advertising, exacerbated by the development of social media algorithms. Besides products and services, we are sold an entitlement to convenience, self-indulgence, and having our every need met. Coupled with the self-interest embedded in capitalism, there is no cultural space left for the common good or community concern except as an individual choice; that is, unless it is in one's own self-interest.[16] I should emphasize that the extreme nature of American individualism today reflects four decades of a laissez-faire political regime, not an inherent fault of markets. The market economies in European social democracies generally do not overwhelm community concern.

The extremes of income inequality and the general meltdown of the social fabric of America over the last four decades have encouraged many economic, political, and social thought leaders to propose a variety of reforms of unregulated capitalism.[17] And no doubt major reforms of free-market capitalism are urgently needed. But how—besides the obvious power struggles to maintain the status quo—to decide among alternative proposals? The role of a moral system like natural humanism is to provide the vision: to articulate the values and goals that any community-concerned economic system must support.

In the present moment, with the climate crisis our overriding concern, the non-negotiable first goal and highest priority of the global community must be to achieve sustainability. How we can begin to do that is the subject of the next chapter. Second in priority only to sustainability is the complementary urgency of social justice, the sum of economic, political, and cultural changes needed to replace the current failed neoliberal global agenda with humanistic institutional and governance systems.

9
LIFE'S LESSONS
FOR SUSTAINABILITY

In Part II, we looked to nature to see how humanity relates to the rest of life on Earth, and to learn from nature what it means to live sustainably; and we identified the functional patterns and principles that account for the biosphere's sustainability. The purpose of this chapter is to distill those insights into *normative* values, goals, and strategies for our species. What does nature tell us about what humanity should do to live sustainably? How must our values and priorities change? What should we aim to accomplish?

I have derived ten Lessons for Sustainability from the patterns and principles identified in chapter seven. The biosphere of today has obviously been impacted by human activity over recent centuries, but its core operating patterns and principles evolved long before human presence was a factor. These patterns and principles are directly observable, reasonably consensual facts; but the lessons I derive from them are not. These ten lessons are how I map life's healthy operating principles into the space of opportunities for human civilization to live and function more sustainably.

Six of these ten lessons concern values and goals to be pursued, including those that address humanity's relationship with planet Earth and those that address people's relationships with each other. The remaining four lessons emphasize strategies and organizing principles. Three of those four illustrate applications of feedback control systems to achieving sustainability in human affairs. The final lesson presents a proposal for constructing an "immune system" for society.

The premise, again, is that the currently entrenched worldwide industrial civilization has begun to destabilize the biosphere, and therefore that humanity is in danger of self-extinction unless we can re-invent our entire economic system with great urgency. The way forward is to reboot our present society as "Civilization 2.0," a new and different version centered on a sustainable way of life. Only a dramatic shift in paradigms—a breakthrough in vision—can achieve so great a transformation quickly enough. What else could be more important?

Relationships: Humanity with Earth and People with Each Other

The first two lessons are established doctrine to the ecologically literate, and are extensively documented, with detailed policies, in sources provided in the Further Reading appendix.[1]

Stewardship: Protect and Care for Planet Earth. For far too long, the idea that *Earth belongs to humans* helped to legitimate an "extractivist" mentality which we must now urgently reverse. At the opposite end of the explanatory spectrum, an ecological stance compels goals at two levels. Humans owe their very existence to the evolution of life on earth through billions of years until higher primate species emerged. Humans survive today only because the biosphere continues to maintain critical conditions for life on earth by regulating oxygen and carbon dioxide levels. Because *humans depend for our very existence on a healthy biosphere,* we are obliged at a minimum to protect it; for our own survival, we should be protecting rather than ravaging our planet and fouling our own nest.

But there is also another level to the ecological mentality, manifested in concepts like reverence, sanctity, and stewardship. These are relationships with nature that go beyond self-interest into a more spiritual realm.[2] As a secular person, I am often overtaken with feelings of awe, reverence, and sanctity while standing at the ocean's shore, or at the foot of a giant redwood tree, or lost in contemplation of how the sun's energy has always sustained all life on earth. How can we not love the enabler and constant protector of all our lives? *How can we not want to take care of the Earth we belong to?* Earth made us, not vice versa. And Earth can easily take us down if we fail to pay our respects. As with any greater power, we can respect out of love or out of fear; what will not wash is humans pretending that we are free to do as we choose!

Energy Efficiency: Conserve, Reuse, Recycle, and Repair. Much of contemporary civilization depends on non-renewable sources of energy, and most products are designed to be used up and discarded; these practices are environmentally destructive and unsustainable. The contemporary concept of sustainability was originally defined in the context of economic development. Sustainable development was conceived as that which satisfies the needs of the present without adversely affecting conditions for future generations. Nature does not make these distinctions. Instead, *nature is intrinsically energy efficient,* relying only on renewable energy sources, and recycling all elements and materials used by living systems. For human civilization to achieve sustainability, we need to adopt the same strategy. We have such a long way to go. We must radically decrease high rates of global extraction, growth, and consumption to very modest levels (by American standards). Reducing global population growth would contribute substantially to decreasing total consumption.

Scientists, policy makers, and many others have known for decades what humanity must do to reduce rising global temperatures and rising sea levels caused by excess carbon dioxide emissions.[3] All uses of fossil fuel energy sources (coal, oil, and natural gas) must end as soon as possible and be replaced by energy from renewable sources (wind, solar, geothermal, and hydroelectric). One major component of achieving this goal is electrifying all means of transportation. Another is rebuilding and renewing all national, state, and local infrastructure with "green" methods. In parallel, we should minimize our total energy use (aka "footprint") by adopting energy efficient technology, practices, and standards everywhere, such as LED technology in lights and screens, all-electric appliances, zero-carbon buildings, and smart energy grids. The mantra remains for all of us to "conserve, reuse, recycle, and repair." Minimizing our ecological footprint is our best strategy to preserve livable conditions for future generations.

The next four lessons provide a road map for how some key aspects of American culture can pivot toward greater sustainability.

Cooperation: Reciprocity and Partnership. Although exceptions abound, hierarchy and domination are the primary organizing principles of the industrial and post-industrial worlds, as well as many cultural institutions throughout history. In *dominator hierarchies*, power and control flow in one direction from top to bottom, from the outrageous extremes of slavery, colonialism, and patriarchy to the petty annoyances of administrative bureaucracies. Recall from chapter five that in biological nature, feedback flows both up and down control hierarchies, all interconnected with each other, so that entire ecosystems can simultaneously maintain their vitality and nimbly adapt to changing conditions. Your brain and nervous system work the same way to attain the same objectives.

To achieve sustainability, *we need to transform our dominator hierarchies into systems that operate by cooperation, reciprocity, and partnership.*[4] Many of us already participate in relationships based on these principles within our immediate families, and within teams devoted to a common outcome at work or play. For anyone socialized into patriarchy or racism, however, dominator habits die extremely hard. As mentioned earlier, dominator belief systems support a primal urge to feel superior to others by treating them as inferior. Part of any transformative social design must be to highlight opportunities for recognition and fulfillment without the need to belittle others. Naturalist and humanist values provide a plethora of those opportunities, beginning with our common interest in survival. Cooperation, reciprocity, and partnership are the sustainable alternatives to domination relationships.

Solidarity: Global Interdependence and Common Interest. For well over a century, and with increased intensity during the last four decades, America's dominant ethos has been a blend of free-market capitalism and radical individualism, fostering an attitude of "me for myself." This attitude is the complete opposite of how we should relate to nature and to each other. In Part II we established that all living things are interconnected in a vast network of feedback loops, creating multiple levels of dependencies among the entities. Humans are not only interdependent with nature but also interdependent with each other. To deeply understand this idea, one must break the habit of assuming that entities are independent objects (the materialist paradigm) and instead learn to pay attention to how all entities are interconnected (the ecological paradigm).[5]

Solidarity is defined as "unity or agreement of feeling or action, especially among individuals with a common interest; mutual support within a group." At its core, the *feeling* of solidarity is familiar to everyone. Most of us feel degrees of solidarity with our immediate families and closest friends. Yet people differ widely in with whom they perceive a common interest, and how they identify with one group or another. Historically, our social worlds have been divided into distinct tribes, religions, and nations; and between the powerful and the powerless. Feelings of solidarity might be more or less strong within one's own group, but nonexistent with outsiders. *What's changed fundamentally with the climate crisis is that for the first time in human history everyone on the planet now has a common interest with everyone else.* These days, historical divisions are obstacles to surmount or transcend, because we surely will face extinction unless we can achieve some level of global solidarity around the climate crisis.

Diversity: Resilience and Pluralism. Unregulated capitalism's singular pursuit of profit, and efficiencies of scale related to profit, inevitably create consolidation of smaller businesses into fewer and larger ones, as well as a relative uniformity of processes and products. These trends are antithetical to resilience, the capacity (of a person or a whole society) to recover quickly and easily from difficulties. Resilience is prevalent in living systems because natural selection favors organisms and processes that can anticipate and respond effectively to indeterminate change.

Nature achieves resilience because of localism and diversity. Recall that species evolve to fit *local* habitats which, collectively, are more diverse than global ones. Localism is one of the principal strategies by which nature achieves diversity. The other principal strategy is sexual reproduction, which assures two different sets of chromosomes in every offspring. Additional means of creating variation include chance mutations, symbiosis, and sundry forms of synergy. In biological nature, *diversity ensures a robust capacity to survive change. Such resilience is an important part of the toolkit humanity needs to achieve sustainability.*

As is true for solidarity, the species-wide climate crisis fundamentally changes the stakes for diversity. Instead of feeling comfortable only in the presence of others "just like us," we all must learn to recognize, appreciate, and embrace the intrinsic benefits of diversity for humanity as a whole. As Gandhi famously put it, "Our ability to reach unity in diversity will be the beauty and the test of our civilization." As we saw in Part I, in the quest for truth, embracing multiple perspectives is the only way to overcome the limitations inherent in each perspective by itself. We need diverse points of view not only to home in on the truth but also to have confidence in the process of truth-seeking and hence in its results. Pluralism is a threat only to people convinced that there can be just one right answer, a dead-end stance in this era of global issues and constant change. In a sustainable society, diversity, pluralism, and multiplicity are virtues to be celebrated as enriching in themselves, and as essential to our shared quest for survival.

Democracy and Generosity. The biosphere operates as a whole system finely tuned to the specific needs of all its living creatures. By regulating oxygen and carbon dioxide levels and, thereby, global temperature, the biosphere ensures the continuity of critical conditions for all life on Earth to survive and flourish. Thus, nature achieves sustainability at all nested levels. The organisms and ecosystems that constitute life on Earth—the entities or "parts" of the biosphere—do not have goals of their own in tension or conflict with the whole system. *Except for human beings*, nothing in nature imagines stepping out of its inherited role. All organisms actively explore their inherited worlds, displaying a plethora of local autonomy, self-expression, and diversity within the constraints of an elegantly coordinated and regulated global regime.

Among nature's more common constraints are limited mating partners and scarce food and water supplies. Under these circumstances, animals must compete for resources, and the fighting can be deadly. Social animals (including humans) also compete among themselves to establish pecking orders. These competitions all serve necessary winnowing or sorting functions within particular contexts but are the exceptions rather than the rule. In nature, the entire web of life exists in dynamic states of mutual support.

Nature's generally harmonious, productive, and sustainable relationship between subordinate elements and the whole biosphere stands in stark contrast to the perpetual conflicts in human affairs between the desires of the few and the interests of the many. *For humanity to achieve sustainability, the domination and exploitation of the powerless by the powerful must be curtailed.* Human nations and states are capable of mutually supportive institutions and governing structures. They are most certainly the exceptions in the world of today, but that fact does not change what nature has to offer us by way of a better example.

A functional human equivalent of how the biosphere operates would be a democratic and benevolent society in which *everyone* is equally entitled to participate in meaningful decision making and to receive safety-net "welfare state" social benefits (shelter, health care, education, and the dignity of useful labor) for life. Nothing is implied about how the economic activity of such a society might be organized to accomplish these purposes. Instead, the point is precisely that the imperatives of economic theories become secondary to the priority of bestowing dignity upon all human beings. (This principle foreshadows the focus of our next chapter, "Humanist Values and Principles.") Needless to say, a political paradigm in which economic ideology is secondary is radically different from persistent Western political thought based on the dogmas of free market capitalism. Instead, the first concern of the humanist paradigm is the unrivaled value of the physical, mental, and emotional well-being of all the people on earth—of humanity at large.

In a benevolent society, the aspect of liberty that matters most is not the "freedom *from*" (restraint or arbitrary control) but rather the "freedom *to*" (become the person you can become). This distinction is sometimes called "positive" freedom versus "negative" freedom. Positive freedom entails meeting everyone's basic needs to assure that opportunities for growth are not stunted before they can start. Everyone is treated humanely and is free to adapt and express themselves *within* the global constraints of norms, incentives, and laws created to foster the society's central moral principles and goals: (1) an overriding commitment to sustainability and (2) universal human rights to shelter, health care, education, and the dignity of useful labor. Such a benevolent society is not plausible without the added assumption of a political regime with *legitimate* authority, meaning a comprehensive and truthful democracy with transparent and accountable government agencies. Clearly, *the entire relationship between individuals and the state is transformed in a fully democratic and benevolent society*.

Feedback Control Systems in Human Affairs

The next three lessons all illustrate applications of feedback control systems to achieving sustainability in human affairs.

Homeostasis: Optimize and Regulate. The goal of sustainability is in direct conflict with the unlimited growth of global population and consumption. Earth's carrying capacity for human beings has likely been exceeded already; it's difficult to know definitively because it depends on the multiplier used to account for our rate of consumption.[6] And no one knows yet how to factor into these calculations the tons of plastics rapidly piling up in the oceans. Suffice it to say, humanity should place a very high priority on limiting further growth of global population and consumption, and urgently prevent any further use of nonbiodegradable plastics, which are slowly poisoning all living creatures. New biodegradable materials are available to be used as substitutes if the right incentives are provided to accelerate their adoption.

However, there is much more to this issue than merely curbing the excesses of the industrial economy. This is not just a one-time correction to an overshoot, only to repeat the pattern again. The far-reaching lesson for humanity is that being constrained by limits is typically a *good* thing, a necessary method of achieving valued outcomes. The deep idea is the contrast between maximizing and optimizing. The finances of capitalism are all about maximizing profit; if anything is good, more is better. But maximizing is not sustainable; it is not how nature operates; and it is rarely how humans should operate. *Nature optimizes.* Nature evolves into systems with optimum dynamic range for each parameter *and* carefully regulates the activity of organisms and ecosystems to stay within those ranges. The tops and bottoms of these dynamic ranges are limits playing a necessary, constructive role in achieving valued outcomes. *This is the basic logic of biological homeostasis, which humans seeking sustainability should emulate whenever possible.*

Adaptability: Organizational Learning. As discussed in Part II, a strikingly powerful and consistent pattern throughout the biosphere is the combination of, and balance between, stability and flexibility. All living systems maintain dynamic stability internally, while continuously adapting to changing external conditions. More highly evolved organisms and ecosystems can adapt to ever wider ranges of circumstances. Higher primates and many other animals continue to learn and adapt to new situations throughout their lifetimes. For the design of human systems—organizations, institutions, policies, and practices—this pattern of balancing stability with flexibility should be an overall goal to be met as well and as often as possible.

For society to operate sustainably, *industrial-era bureaucratic structures and practices need to be transformed into more open, flexible, dynamic systems.* Some progress in this direction has already occurred in so-called "data-driven" or organizational learning practices adopted by progressive leaders in business and education. Essentially, small groups at every organizational level repeat regular cycles of (a) setting collective goals, (b) implementing those goals, (c) gathering data to determine whether the goals are being met, (d) reviewing this information as a group, and (e) revisiting the goals, how to achieve them, and how to measure them. Note that these cycles of feedback and adjustment are perfect analogs of the basic "control system" unit of biosphere self-regulation at the core of nature's sustainability.

As a pioneer in human systems design, Peter Senge began beating the "learning organization" drum over thirty years ago.[7] When implemented effectively, learning organizations develop the capacity to evolve with changing conditions. However, this kind of transformation only succeeds in organizations with a climate of trust and legitimacy, which implies organizational transparency and accountability. *More transparent and accountable state and federal governance must be a very high priority*, as a critical step on the path to major organizational reform of industrial-era bureaucracies into more dynamic, adaptive systems.

Regulation: Achieving Desired Outcomes. In nature, regulation is central and essential to life itself, from single cells to the entire biosphere. Each organism maintains itself as conditions change by virtue of its homeostatic regulation. The whole web of living systems is interconnected with feedback loops, so events that deviate from expected ranges at any level of a complex system are noted as such, and signals are sent up and down the hierarchy of levels as needed to accommodate them. You may recognize this picture of regulation as the way your nervous system works.

By contrast, in states and countries with market economies, regulation typically means action taken to compensate for unwanted market results. Economists presume the market is always the ideal method to allocate resources. In tandem with the American ethos of radical individualism, non-regulation is an important default principle. In this context, regulation is seen as an intervention necessitated by "market failure." Clearly, this economic concept of regulation bears little relation to how regulation functions in nature.

The difference is that the overriding goal in nature is to stay alive—a *universal* value—and that the same basic system of regulation has been built into the structure of life from the beginning. The overriding goal of a capitalist market system, by contrast, is to accrue profit to the lenders and owners of capital by any means necessary. The achievement of other worthy goals (such as healthy air and water, decent working conditions and a living wage, or consumer protection from fraud) is left to "market forces," unless the economic system is forcefully and persistently constrained by laws and regulations designed to achieve such goals. In contrast to the harmony and alignment of goals in non-human nature, an intrinsic conflict exists between *unregulated* capitalism and the health and welfare of humanity as a whole, as well as the planet itself.

Recall that regulation in nature is enacted by self-correcting feedback systems, while growth is enacted by self-amplifying feedback systems. From outside the perspective of capitalist ideology, it is obvious that uncontrolled growth is both dangerous and unsustainable. Stabilizing regulation uses feedback to keep any function or behavior within prescribed limits; that is, to constrain the process from deviating too far from the specified target. By defining a goal in terms of a parameter and then comparing the outcome with the value of that parameter, *regulation is nature's proven, definitive method for achieving specified values, goals, and purposes.*

A nation with a clear idea of its goals should concern itself first with how best to achieve them, not with how they might affect corporate profits. Consider how the U.S. military is under civilian command to ensure that its actions are guided by the nation's priorities. By analogy, the economy should also be subordinate to overriding national goals. Along with familiar incentives, *an abundant use of regulation is a compelling strategy to obtain desired sustainability outcomes,* consigning economic policy to a secondary, supportive role. Instead of asking *how much* regulation is good for the economy, we should ask, What kind of regulation is best suited to achieve sustainability quickly? How do we express these goals in parameters we can measure? What numerical values do we assign to those parameters?

A Societal "Immune System"

The final lesson consists of a proposal for a built-in "immune system" for society.

Built-in Safeguards: Society's Immune System. In nature, safeguards against threats are built into the very fabric of life. Not so in culture. If we aspire to live sustainably, it will be necessary to build robust safeguards right into the heart of our cultures.

Nature's built-in safeguards evolved and were optimized over eons of biological time. Life's overriding goals are survival and reproduction. Living systems die if their internal milieu is not maintained within critical levels; thus, homeostasis is the first line of defense against many deadly internal threats. External threats from microbial pathogens are countered with immune systems which, in higher animals, create future immunity after exposure to specific pathogens. Besides fighting diseases from bacteria and viruses, human immune systems form the first line of defense against many early forms of cancer, recognizing the transformed cells as "one of them" rather than "one of us." And during early stages of development, most embryos or fetuses with critical abnormalities are naturally aborted.

Because cultures are constructed by humans, the main threats and dangers to cultures are what humans do to themselves (and the planet). The only source of safeguards against what humans do to themselves are those very same humans. Unlike the foregoing lessons of this chapter, in the matter of safeguards, the mapping from biology to culture is unclear. The essential message is that we must build in our own safeguards, but the particular dangers and their appropriate safeguards have yet to be identified. One proposal for constructing a pertinent "social immune system" follows.

First is the need to specify what overriding cultural goals might be in danger. If survival and reproduction are life's ultimate purposes, on what basis could any comparison be drawn with culture or society? In the context of natural humanism, I imagine a purposeful community of nations committed to sustainability. Living sustainably would require a higher order of global cooperation, coordination, and continuity of purpose than humanity has so far managed to achieve. Evidence of such a focused commitment to a common interest also implies some level of success in disarming the disruptive forces of extreme inequalities, racism, and destructive ideological conflicts. This conception of society incorporates many of this chapter's lessons, and it captures my idea of what needs protection: the basic integrity of such a purposeful community. This kind of community should attempt to build safeguards into its very fabric to protect itself from known and hypothetical threats to its basic integrity. The same line of thought should apply as well to a purposeful community within a single nation.

Many of the greatest sources of danger have been recognized for centuries (and often ascribed to excessive testosterone), including perennial vices like lust and greed, premeditated violence, and notable concentrations of power in any sphere of influence.[8] Another more recently recognized class of threats derives from cognitive biases and illusions (like confirmation bias, loss aversion, groupthink, wishful thinking and denial) and emotional needs for certainty (fundamentalist and totalitarian ideologies). By these means people create specious belief systems and use them to legitimate antisocial behavior. Combinations of both classes of these dangers can produce political regimes analogous to cancer in biological systems, wherein runaway corruption destroys governing capacity from within, seen most recently in the United States during the Trump administration.

A different class of dangers lurks in the enduring preoccupation of many people to transcend human limitations through a liberating technology, be it medical or computational. Excluded from this category is space exploration, which of necessity respects human biological, mental and social limits every step of the way. My concern is exemplified by the 21st century technological infatuation with artificial intelligence. Proselytizers who characterize AI algorithms as primed to revolutionize society are fooling themselves and their followers by ignoring the fact that these algorithms have always simply done the bidding of their creators. First, AI algorithms don't work at all like human brains, which are largely analog, fully integrated into human bodies, and specialized to create a workable sense of reality for humans to interact with. Digital algorithms can never, *in principle*, create *meaningful* contexts the way human brains do. Second, the most impressive feats of AI algorithms have always been, and remain, outperforming humans on specific tasks for which they have been trained, one way or another. Claims to have exceeded this limited scope of achievement are marketing hype or fantasies which ultimately pose a threat to a humanistic, sustainable society.[9]

The best way to protect society from these and innumerable other dangers is to build sustainable communities so strongly and effectively as to keep threats and dangers marginalized. To me, this is the true mapping of nature's strategy of building protections into the very fabric of life. If the essential fabric of culture consists of commitments to democracy, science, and diversity/pluralism, these practices in tandem will function as society's "immune system"; neither internal nor external threats will have much success in disrupting it. Only to the extent that these pillars are undermined (i.e., the immune system is compromised), will society have to shift its priorities to an additional full-bore defense.

Democracy as a first principle means a hearty implementation of "a government for, by, and of the people." For starters: everyone votes conveniently and reliably; the electoral college is abolished and gerrymandering forbidden; and all elections are entirely publicly funded, resulting in strict limits on time allowed for campaigning. Another necessity is constitutional repeal of Citizens United and personhood for corporations. Media should be required to establish some firewall between news and entertainment to insulate news from the profit motive, protecting citizens' rights to be well-informed with useful, factual journalism. In such a true democratic context, cultural norms would support inclusive and meaningful policy deliberations, and the complementary first principles of science and diversity would be embraced enthusiastically.

Science as a first principle means a deep commitment to the authority of skeptical empiricism, not any particular set of facts. It means significant funding for teaching at all levels, for critical thinking skills and statistical literacy, and for continuing ecological education for adults; and heavy reliance on scientific expertise in government policy, including public health, and social science advice on negotiating and decision-making (especially how to encourage creativity and avoid "groupthink.") Unlike today, when economic ideology and technological futurism saturate public discourse, we would expect to see a plethora of public debate on policy issues raised by concerns for sustainability and how to guide cultural evolution. A commitment to science will also serve to legitimate the first principles of democracy and diversity.

Diversity as a first principle means a deep commitment to its intrinsic value in every facet of life. It means pluralism, as in multiple perspectives brought to bear on all significant political and social issues. It means a bias toward variation and multiplicity in everything from products and companies to cuisines and the arts. It means prejudice against all concentrations of power—a disposition to rein them in before they can establish themselves—with strong legal protection against monopolies. It means aggressive laws and policies against discrimination based on race, ethnicity, gender, or sexual identity. With this mindset, the energy otherwise dissipated on identity and racial politics would be freed up to promote the solidarity of "unity in diversity."

It bears emphasis that a bias toward variation and multiplicity, together with a prejudice against all concentrations of power—which would reverse the opposite trends of the neoliberal regime—would restore the autonomy of local communities and smaller cultural groups to create their own solutions to economic, social, and political problems. For example, in finance, we would see a return to Main Street together with the curtailment of Wall Street.[10] And who does not prefer the quality of food from local farmers' markets to that of global supply chains?!

I contend that in a community bound to democracy, science, and diversity as first principles, threats and dangers to a cohesive, purposeful body politic would not be able to grab a toehold. Besides their intrinsic benefits, these practices in tandem constitute a social immune system. Not that this is the whole story, of course. It follows that these very "first principles" will be under constant challenge from those committed to the old order, anxious to retain or recover their previous power. That points to the need to keep the social immune system robust—we must, indeed, provide safeguards for the safeguards.

At the conclusion of chapter seven (Nature's Healthy Operating Principles), I briefly highlighted three dimensions of fundamental conflict between industrial civilization and sustainability: Time Scale, Unconstrained Growth, and Domination. These highlights implicitly posed questions which this chapter begins to address. Stewardship and energy efficiency are steps in the right direction toward a sustainable balance between present and future needs. The amplifying feedback loop of unconstrained growth is a cancer that must be cut out of the heart of our civilization immediately. The "cure," as nature shows us, is to use regulation's stabilizing feedback principle as the foremost strategy and means of accomplishing our goals. In one way or another, we can begin to see purposeful regulation as the antidote to unconstrained growth.

Diversity and solidarity offer alternative organizational strategies to domination hierarchies. The depth of emotional attachment so many people have to religious and racial ideologies—built on domination hierarchies—is an undeniable stumbling block for any movement promoting common interests across these lines. If the climate crisis ultimately gets the better of humanity, I would bet on race or religious fault lines being the culprit rather than capital investment. Still, the bottom line now is human survival, and we all have a common interest in that!

I have tipped my cards early on the "first principles" of democracy, science, and diversity. Future criteria for progress should be more about achieving sustainability and humanistic goals than about benchmarks for gross output. Two chapters ahead, we will look at "intentional" or "managed" cultural evolution as one way to frame the whole process of *continuous improvement*, an obvious choice to replace quantitative growth as the measure of our collective efficacy.

10
HUMANIST VALUES AND PRINCIPLES

The possibility of species-wide destruction creates for the first time the necessity of a species-wide ethic.

— **Al Gore (1992)**[1]

Humanism is a broad and far-reaching philosophy with a long history deserving more extensive treatment than this chapter offers. My limited purpose here is to continue to flesh out the moral principles of natural humanism from a humanist perspective. My version of humanism is in harmony with its core principles, but departs from tradition in two significant respects. Believing in constructionism and pluralism, I emphasize the need to incorporate multiple perspectives into normative decision making to enhance its legitimacy; and I maintain a specifically contemporary focus on the climate crisis, sustainability, and the dangers of unregulated capitalism.

The Health, Well-Being, and Fulfillment of All Human Beings

The moral essence of humanism is the bold assertion that our social, political, and economic institutions, including our norms and belief systems, should promote and celebrate the health, well-being, and fulfillment of all human beings. One might wish this assertion were self-evident, but of course human history proves otherwise. Kings and autocrats, colonialists and patriarchs, and most global corporations support and benefit from institutions that privilege elites, exploit everyone else, and legitimate existing "inequality regimes"[2] through doctrines and ideologies that disempower most of world's population. By continuing to destabilize the earth's biosphere, the contemporary neoliberal regime of unregulated capitalism actually poses a direct threat to human survival. The worldview of Natural Humanism presented here is close to the antithesis of neoliberalism.

Natural humanist values are grounded in the evolutionary inheritance we share with our fellow social animals. Some of this inheritance is fixed into the structures of our brains and bodies, but most of what we inherit are predispositions, ready to be molded into fully functioning members of society through culturally-specific interactions with caregivers and a larger circle of other humans. This dichotomy between biology and culture harkens back to the duality of the human condition discussed in chapter one. Moral systems provide the values and principles that give meaning and direction to the ongoing cultural co-construction process.

All moral systems have three similar components. First are the core *premises* that require the attention and direction delivered by the moral code. For example, the Catholic doctrine of original sin is what dictates the necessity of salvation. A core premise of natural humanism, as described in chapter eight, is that humans inherit the same basic emotional makeup as other social animals. Second are the *ideal states* or conditions toward which the moral code points. In natural humanism, the broad, generic concepts of health, well-being, and fulfillment represent optimum conditions, assuming that more specific goals or conditions will be specified as needed to suit local customs or for specific purposes. Third are the *values and principles* deemed necessary to achieve the ideal conditions, given the stated premises.

The focus of this chapter is on humanist values and principles, including the societal conditions needed to achieve (reasonable levels of) health, well-being, and fulfillment for all human beings. I will discuss these values in the context of our evolutionary inheritance because the *legitimacy* of humanist values rests on an accurate and convincing explication of its premises. Values and principles are embraced in direct proportion to the acceptance of the premises on which they are based.

If a human characteristic is fixed and permanent, society must constitute itself wisely to make the best of it. If it is universal (species-wide), conclusions drawn about it apply to everyone. Thus, inevitability and universality have always carried the greatest weight in legitimating any moral system. Our genetic predispositions are both inevitable and universal; however, they are far from lifetime sentences. Biological predispositions are more like default tendencies, leaving lots of room for adaptation and customization. Natural humanism seeks to capitalize on these available degrees of freedom to achieve humanist ideals through the design and construction of cultural practices and institutions.

In order to determine which societal conditions would be most favorable to the achievement of (reasonable levels of) health, well-being, and fulfillment for everyone, we need a proper understanding of what is fixed through inheritance. Specifically, we need to identify which inherited characteristics deserve special attention and direction from a moral system, and what makes them special. *What conditions do people really need to live a life worth living?* Here is how I see it:

All humans inherit basic needs for bodily health, physical and mental safety, and interpersonal bonding. They are also instinctively curious, seeking to explore and manipulate their immediate environment. In addition, humans demonstrate the same intrinsic autonomy, self-determination, and agency as all other living creatures. These three sets of characteristics are my premises in the moral logic of this chapter. Despite the fact that they are integrated together in each human being, I treat them separately in the following discussion because they figure into society as if they were three distinct, complementary dimensions. In brief:

- Basic needs are generally understood to be universal human requirements that families or the community should provide for everyone, but the matter of who bears the financial and social responsibility for meeting these needs is perennially contested on ideological grounds.

- Instinctive curiosity is the root of our motivation to acquire knowledge and practical skills, and to be a competent person in society. Society's role is to provide the opportunities to learn and to participate in meaningful work, which entails the moral imperative to achieve equality of those opportunities through inclusion, distributive fairness, and due process.

- Autonomy, self-determination, and agency are universal, primal instincts at the heart of political demands for freedom and the moral imperative of democracy. Representation is not sufficient for self-governance; participation and agency are essential as well.

These aspects of human inheritance demand our moral attention because of the profound harm suffered from their neglect, as well as the great benefits to be reaped from their proper support. They are the characteristics of our evolutionary heritage that offer the greatest leverage in achieving widespread health, well-being, and fulfillment. One might even call them keys to unlocking human potential. They are linchpins of natural humanistic values and principles. Let us now consider these three aspects in greater depth.

Basic Needs

The full range of humanist values encompasses desires and interests as well as needs, but needs have moral priority because they are necessary rather than discretionary. Humans have needs (i.e., requirements) because we are made (by evolution) to operate (interact) in environments with particular physical and social characteristics, and because we develop step by step from helpless infants into functioning adults. By definition, needs are not optional; they are necessary for a host of immutable reasons, such as our inherited emotional makeup, the unavoidable demands of participating in society, or the fated consequences of the life cycle. For example, we must all learn how to inhibit certain impulses to be able to get along with other people. By contrast, desires and interests are discretionary—wishes or wants rather than needs—no matter how intense and powerful the associated urges may be.

The conception of basic needs best suited to our discussion comes from a theory developed in the mid-20th century by the clinical psychologist Abraham Maslow.[3] Maslow conceives of basic needs in terms of social development. He blends biology and culture seamlessly and organizes the basic needs insightfully, helping us see which societal conditions would neglect or support them. His theory posits five broad categories of basic needs in a hierarchy of ascending levels, wherein higher levels emerge only after lower levels of needs are gratified. Of the five levels, only the three lower ones relate to our concerns here.[4]

- *The Physiological Needs* comprise: (a) critical levels of all the homeostatic chemical and physical parameters discussed in chapter five [e.g., oxygen, water, nutrition]; (b) sleep, activity, and exercise; (c) sensory pleasures [e.g., tastes, smells, touching]; and (d) sexual gratification.

- *The Safety Needs* comprise: (a) security and stability; (b) protection and freedom from fear, anxiety, and chaos; and (c) structure, laws, and limits. In Maslow's words,[5] *the average child and, less obviously, the average adult in our society generally prefers a safe, orderly, predictable, lawful, organized world, which he can count on and in which unexpected, unmanageable, chaotic, and other dangerous things do not happen, and in which, in any case, he has powerful parents or protectors who shield him from harm. …The tendency to have some world religion or philosophy that organizes the universe and the people in it into some sort of satisfactorily coherent, meaningful whole is also in part motivated by safety seeking.*

- *The Belongingness and Love Needs* comprise: (a) identifying as part of a family, group, clan, gang, or other close-knit community, neighborhood, or territory; and (b) companionship, contact, intimacy, and affectionate relationships with friends, sweethearts, spouses, children, or animals.

This high-level summary of basic needs covers quite a broad range, from lifelong bodily needs to identity issues most prominent during teenage and young adult years. Yet common to the very notion of basic needs is the sense that one could suffer harm from being deprived of their satisfaction, especially at an early age or for long periods of time.[6] Satisfying needs is always a matter of degree, as typically designated by words like "minimal," "sufficient," "optimal," and "maximum." What is minimal for one person or one situation might be sufficient for another (and vice versa). Also, consider that development is *inherently* sequential. We must learn to stand before we can learn to walk. Infants are programmed to entice others to interact with and care for them. What comes next inevitably depends on how the previous stage went. For many people, having needs met poorly early in life sets a permanent upper bound on what they can ever achieve. For just this reason, *meeting basic needs early in life has the greatest leverage to minimize preventable social pathologies and therefore to advance social justice.*

The values and practices most conducive to meeting basic needs throughout the lifespan are *caring relationships* and the nurturing environments they sustain. As political theorist Joan Tronto writes, "Care is about meeting needs, and it is always *relational*: the skinned knee of a child who fell off his bike isn't only about scrapes and germs, it is also about creating the conditions for him to feel safe in the world."[7] Caring relationships encompass *attention* to needs, *responsibility* for meeting needs, the actual work of *caregiving*, and being *responsive* to its results. Caring manifests empathy and demands competence. Caring is deeply embedded in our evolutionary history and is a core humanist value.

Of course, we aim to achieve not only an absence of social pathologies, but also an abundance of well-being and fulfillment. From the cross-disciplinary perspective of "Prevention Science," *nurturing environments* are the best means to both ends. Decades of prevention research can be summed up in the following four highly successful strategies of nurturing environments: (1) reduce coercion, (2) reinforce prosocial behavior, (3) limit negative influences and opportunities, and (4) promote psychological flexibility.[8] Caring and nurturing might as well be synonyms; the values, dispositions, and behaviors that best meet basic human needs flow from the same inherited instincts and impulses. And, unsurprisingly, the best way to reduce social pathology is to optimize well-being.

The importance of reducing coercion deserves special emphasis. In this context coercion refers to "the use of aversive behavior in an attempt to terminate someone else's aversive behavior."[9] We all recognize the habit of threatening to punish someone who is behaving badly. No doubt counteraggression evolved culturally because of survival value; and it has persisted because it can sometimes be effective in the short run. But *coercion is the behavioral pattern at the root of all conflict*. The caring, nurturant alternative to coercion is *forbearance*, meaning patient self-control, restraint, and tolerance. Forgiveness, empathy, and compassion are the other prominent nurturant values and dispositions. As prevention guru Anthony Biglan puts it, "every time we influence someone to replace coercive reactions with behavior that calms and supports others, we have one more person who is cultivating these same nurturing reactions in those around them."[10]

Words like "compassion," "forbearance," "caring," and "nurturance" refer to humanist values, dispositions, and behaviors, but these terms need to be translated and mapped on to discrete family or social services to figure into the policy discourse of political economy. When states and politicians want to accomplish goals, they create appropriate programs and legislate funding for them. The proper response of a state to the moral imperative of meeting basic human needs is to enact and generously fund extensive health, education, and family-social support legislation.

Sadly, under the neoliberal (minimal government) regime in America, caregiving in all respects has been largely relegated to the private sector or individual families, resulting in massive inequalities. Only the wealthy can afford to pay for quality childcare or long-time support for elderly family members. In fact, absent exorbitant prices, there is an inherent, unavoidable conflict between any kind of quality care and a decent profit. In short, neoliberalism has effectively broken caregiving in

America. By 2020, a progressive political movement had begun to coalesce around the concept of Universal Family Care, which encompasses preschool and daycare services, paid family and medical leave, and medical and non-medical caregiving for seniors or people with disabilities. The most likely funding approach would be a social insurance program in the vein of Medicare and Social Security.[11]

A Universal Family Care program may still be a long shot in America, but elsewhere in the world, meeting the gamut of basic human needs is considered a moral obligation in tandem with other universal human rights. For instance, the United Nations' 1948 Universal Declaration of Human Rights, Article 25 characterizes this moral obligation as "social protection":[12]

(1) Everyone has the right to a standard of living adequate for the health and well-being of himself [sic] and of his family, including food, clothing, housing and medical care and necessary social services, and the right to security in the event of unemployment, sickness, disability, widowhood, old age or other lack of livelihood in circumstances beyond his [sic] control.

(2) Motherhood and childhood are entitled to special care and assistance. All children, whether born in or out of wedlock, shall enjoy the same social protection.

This declaration, that *everyone has the right to this scope of social protection*, is the clearest statement I can find of what I called a "benevolent" society in the previous chapter. In today's world, the closest actual approximations to this ideal are social democracies in Western Europe, where political programs and funding partially reflect a cultural ethos that everyone has an equal right to social benefits that ensure their well-being.

Instinctive Curiosity

Instinctive curiosity is the root of our motivation to acquire knowledge and practical skills, and to be a competent person in society. Recall from chapter eight that humans inherit the same emotionally-driven social behaviors as other *primates* because we share similar subcortical brain structures that control emotions unconsciously via neurotransmitters and hormones such as dopamine, serotonin, oxytocin, and endorphins. The origins of instinctive curiosity go even deeper into evolutionary history, to a suite of primal emotional systems we share with all *mammals*.

By the time mammals evolved, their subcortical brain regions had differentiated into distinct systems producing well-organized, survival-oriented behavior sequences in response to relevant inputs. The research program of affective neuroscientist Jaak Panksepp established that all mammal brains contain seven such primal emotional systems, which he designated with capital letters to distinguish his use of these words from other meanings.[13]

- The FEAR (escape) system causes freezing or flight, to minimize the chances of bodily destruction.

- The RAGE (attack) system energizes the body to angrily defend its territory and resources.

- The PANIC (crying) system generates feelings of grief, sadness, and "separation distress" from social loss.

- The LUST (sexual) system leads males and females to potential mates and reproduction.

- The CARE (maternal) system motivates the nurturing of offspring, for as long as it takes.

- The PLAY (social) system stimulates rough-and-tumble interactions among young animals to help them learn basic social and survival skills.

- The SEEKING (expectancy) system "makes animals intensely interested in exploring their world and leads them to get excited when they are about to get what they desire."

We encounter the simple form of the SEEKING system when dogs or squirrels move forward, sniff, and energetically investigate their surroundings. *SEEKING is the emotional foundation of curiosity and the purposeful exploration of our physical and social worlds that all human beings do spontaneously.* The evolutionary origin of SEEKING in mammalian brains was the survival benefit of learning how to fully exploit local environmental resources; the contemporary human equivalent is the need to develop a suite of mental, social, and emotional skills to navigate and discover a viable path through the thicket of challenges and opportunities that life affords.

The core behaviors that emanate from SEEKING are curiosity, exploration, and manipulation of entities to discover their properties—quintessentially *general* activities, as applicable to symbolic domains as physical ones. These behaviors are effective means to any number of important ends. In fact, SEEKING behaviors are the epitome of ends in their own right, what psychologists often call "intrinsically" motivated behavior.[14] The most direct result of these activities is the accumulation of knowledge, a very broad concept that encompasses skills and experience as well as facts about the world. However, the brain did not evolve to acquire knowledge for its own sake; its primary role continues to be to make sense of the world in the service of bodily and emotional needs. If the ultimate purpose of the SEEKING system is to enable the organism to take effective action in the world, the best word to capture that result is "competence," the objective sense of the word, which also implies readiness, ability, and mastery. That is the essence of what SEEKING behaviors produce, as well as the social and cultural benefits of having achieved such mastery.

When children's instincts to explore and master the world are properly nurtured, they are being prepared to become lifelong learners and self-directed participants in opportunities to fulfill their personal goals and to contribute to collective self-governance. By contrast, when these instincts are neglected or thwarted, children's horizons and ambitions are severely diminished. *The humanist ideals of well-being and fulfillment are at stake in this contrast.* The difference between nurturing and neglecting these instincts in the first few years of childhood rests primarily on parents, but after that it depends on what opportunities a society provides for learning, broadly construed, and for participating in meaningful work and community affairs.

There are countless opportunities for learning at home any time a teaching-oriented adult interacts with a motivated child around language and word usage, observational skills, or how things work, to pick a few obvious examples. But for most young people in America, formal schooling provides the best opportunity to develop their mental and social capacities. Most children require significant, structured instructional time to master skills or bodies of knowledge like reading and mathematics. Unfortunately, mainstream American culture has always had an anti-intellectual bias; as a result, teachers are severely undervalued and underpaid. Most students in American classrooms never experience learning-by-doing, learning by (more than rote) problem solving, or learning to think critically. With some exceptions in wealthy enclaves, students leave school in America knowing virtually nothing about how our government functions or even how to be thoughtful consumers, let alone such vital 21st century subjects as evolution, ecology, and how to recognize misinformation in social media.

The current employment situation is equally dire. Prior to the neoliberal political regime, most American workers in manufacturing jobs could support their family and identify with a local workplace community, thereby deriving meaning and dignity from their job. These days, with global corporations moving production to countries with lower labor costs, automation replacing many blue-collar jobs, and the disappearance of private sector labor unions, meaningful manufacturing jobs have virtually disappeared. Taking their place are temporary, flexible jobs or service jobs with minimal salaries and no benefits. Workers are increasingly treated by global enterprises as interchangeable, if still a necessary cost of business.

The upshot is that most Americans suffer harm from neglect of developing their capacities as humans. After 40 years of neoliberal ideology, with mindless consumerism encouraged and critical thinking in retreat, and a plurality of low-information, low-wage service providers doing the nation's "essential" work, it is no wonder that drug abuse and suicides keep increasing.[15] Even more dispiriting are inequalities that shift the burdens of neglect to those who can least afford to bear them. These include institutional biases against women, dark skin color, and labor unions. There are two distinct moral imperatives in this situation. The first is to greatly improve the quality of educational and employment opportunities for everyone. The second is to achieve equality of those opportunities through inclusion, distributive fairness, and due process. Neither of these goals can be met without very significant public financial investment.

Autonomy, Self-Determination, and Agency

Autonomy, self-determination, and agency are universal, primal instincts at the heart of political demands for freedom and the moral imperative of democracy. People thrive and experience swells of positive emotion when they can act as self-determining agents. But established centers of power have their own agendas. Totalitarian regimes suppress and obstruct these primal instincts by design; and inept or misguided bureaucracies often manage to impede them unintentionally. Everyone—individuals, tribes, and nations alike—becomes fearful, angry, and/or depressed when these primal instincts are thwarted. Thus, human well-being and fulfillment depend critically on social and political conditions that preserve and support the exercise of autonomy, self-determination, and agency.

Autonomy means *being able to act on your own*, without another person or thing controlling you. A puppet has zero autonomy, but all organisms are inherently autonomous. Self-determination means *making choices for yourself*, without external pressure. Choosing your own college major or entry-level job aims you in one potentially consequential direction rather than another. Autonomy and self-determination are different, complementary expressions of independence from external rule or control and, as such, are among the basic elements of freedom.

Agency means *being able to make something happen*, to produce a result, to be the cause of an effect. It is about the capacity to influence outcomes. Self-determination may or may not imply agency; there is great agency in the choice of a spouse but little agency in the choice of what to have for dinner. Similarly, agency may or may not imply autonomy. Agents enacting their own goals are autonomous; agents following someone else's instructions are not.

A person's beliefs about their own self-determination and agency are consequential and can be influenced by their life circumstances. The critical factor is what you believe to be true about yourself. Mimicking the role of an observer, people often (unconsciously) infer their own internal conditions and capabilities from what they believe to be true about their circumstances.

For example, parents often pressure their children to choose one academic course over another. Consider Sue and Mary, sisters subject to the same entreaties from their parents. Both sisters choose the same academic course they would have chosen without parental involvement. However, Sue feels the pressure keenly while Mary shrugs it off. As a result, Mary will believe she made the course decision by and for herself, while Sue will attribute her decision to the pressure she felt from her parents. Suppose this pattern repeats itself for years. Other factors being equal, the sisters will develop very different images of themselves. Mary will come to see herself as self-determining, while Sue will feel at the mercy of others. These discrepant self-images will have significant, global effects on their future behaviors.[16]

The attribution process involved in self-determination also applies to most other aspects of our self-image, including the subjective experience of agency (aka "self-efficacy"). Beliefs about your capacity to influence outcomes that matter to you can spell the difference between joyful optimism and hopeless pessimism. *Beliefs in our own capabilities are self-fulfilling.* People with a strong sense of self-efficacy are ready to take on the world. Those who doubt their self-efficacy are unlikely to persevere in the face of obstacles to achieving their goals.[17]

Because autonomy, self-determination, and agency are holistic properties—pertaining to the person as a whole—they are of critical importance to (whole) communities and nations as well as individuals. After all, what was The Declaration of the "unalienable Rights [of] Life, Liberty and the pursuit of Happiness" if not the insistent demand of an entire nation for the moral and legal imperatives of autonomy, self-determination, and agency? The Declaration of Independence is an apt point of reference because the social and political conditions necessary to preserve and support autonomy, self-determination, and agency are 21st century updates to the spirit of that moment. In a nutshell, these conditions are everyone's equal right *not to be coerced by physical force, poverty, or hidden manipulation.* The same rights are claimed for individuals, groups, tribes, and nations, to be free of coercion from higher levels of governing organizations.

Coercion by physical force refers to abusive acts of the government, such as police brutality or apprehension of undocumented immigrants, as well as assault, battery, and sexual harassment by individuals. Coercion by poverty is shorthand for the principle that lack of wealth must not be allowed to deny individuals access to social, political, or legal services of any kind. Coercion by hidden manipulation aims to outlaw technologies (including algorithms) that manipulate attention or limit accessibility to information without the subject's awareness, as well as business models that operate social networks on the same intermittent reinforcement principles as Las Vegas slot machines.[18]

Conflicts are inevitable between the desires of self-determining individuals and the best interests of the community as a whole (aka the "common good"). When social action for the common good is required, the eternal questions are, How to create and inculcate the requisite norms and laws, and how to enforce them? There will always be some circumstances where coercion is unavoidable. In chapter eight, for example, we noted the need for selective punishment at certain key points in child rearing. Other prominent examples are the need for enforcement of public safety laws by fines and sentences, public education attendance requirements, and the enforcement of public health orders, such as to wear face masks in public, so wantonly and tragically ignored by millions of individuals during the COVID-19 pandemic.

Only democratic deliberation can claim legitimate authority for reconciling interests of individuals with the common good. Democracy's unique moral status flows directly from the values of autonomy, self-determination, and agency; that is, from its core identity as *self-governance*. As implied by "government of the people, by the people, and for the people," representation in itself does not suffice for self-governance; participation and agency are essential as well. To the extent that citizens participate in government and can bring about meaningful results by their efforts, democracy not only supports but also exemplifies the values of autonomy, self-determination, and agency at the community level. Fully implemented with commitment, democracy also encompasses strong protections against corruption in the form of transparency, accountability, due process, and equal justice in law enforcement.

To recapitulate, humanist values aim to promote and celebrate the health, well-being, and fulfillment of all human beings equally, and to achieve humanist ideals through the design and construction of cultural practices and institutions. Basic needs, instinctive curiosity, and the triad of autonomy, self-determination, and agency demand our moral attention because of the harm suffered from their neglect, as well as the great benefits to be reaped from their proper support. As such, they are the characteristics of our evolutionary heritage that offer the greatest leverage in achieving widespread health, well-being, and fulfillment.

11
TOWARD A NATURAL HUMANIST SOCIETY

The moral problem is that of modifying the factors which now influence future results.

– John Dewey (1922)[1]

Here, I draw on the values and principles of natural humanism to offer implications, concepts, and strategies for institutions, policies, and practices at a general level. To be carried out successfully, broad concepts and strategies such as these must always be adapted to culturally-specific history and circumstances. Ideally, my proposals would be transformed into a variety of culturally-specific policies and practices through democratic deliberation, because such participatory decision processes would engender the greatest buy-in and legitimacy of their outcomes.

One cannot imagine truly significant institutional changes without corresponding changes in worldview (or mindset, or beliefs—pick your terminology). All the changes put forward in this chapter presuppose at least some shift in mindset. At the same time, all significant shifts in mindset are triggered by at least some change(s) in behavior that challenge prior assumptions. Which comes first? Sometimes one, sometimes the other. Beliefs and behaviors are intrinsically linked to each other like dance partners; both develop and emerge out of their mutual interplay.

Recall from chapter three that humans effectively *live* within their belief systems. Most of us compartmentalize our lives and therefore live within more than one belief system at a time. The same is true for companies, tribes, and nations. Typically, one relatively dominant paradigm or belief system is being legitimated continuously to assure everyone that the trains still run on time. But at least one competing theory of what is "really" going on is always circulating among skeptics—just as individuals carry on within their dominant worldview while occasionally harboring doubts about it.

So at least two things are true at once: (a) it is notoriously difficult to bring about large-scale change in the dominant belief system of individuals and nations alike; and (b) there are always cracks in the foundation at the ready to be exploited if circumstances conspire to necessitate a challenge to the status quo. I proceed with the understanding that the changes contemplated in this chapter envision what *could* occur, supposing sufficient shifts in mindset of a critical mass of citizens.

As a first step, consider that a meaningful change in worldview produces significant effects in its own right. A new perspective brings changes in outlook, desires, expectations, goals, and values. A society's norms, expressed as values, function as parameters in its legitimation control system. All through society, conversations small and large will have a different quality when the status quo worldview has been disrupted with a different point of view and new justifications. Another direct effect of changes in citizens' outlook and values is to push the political dynamic in Congress toward the new values (upward causation). Of course, the donor class will continue to exert pressure (downward causation) on Congress to resist changes in policies that benefit the wealthy.

Cultural Evolution

The concept of cultural evolution holds the promise of providing a crucial scaffold or catalyst for a shift in mindset from neoliberalism to natural humanism.

Cultural evolution follows the same basic variation-selection-inheritance logic as biological evolution. Many cultural niches encourage innovation and variety. Although most new songs, new products, new businesses, and new ideas are soon forgotten, the ones that work best and fit the Zeitgeist of the moment stick around for a while. The ones that work best over longer periods of time become absorbed into the culture and interconnected within its ecology. In short, *what works and fits, persists*. Scholars of evolution continue to debate about the specific mechanisms and theoretical status of cultural inheritance.[2] However, there is no doubt that our present variety and complexity of world-wide cultures evolved from simpler hunter-gatherer cultures, and that the process of cultural evolution is ongoing and ubiquitous, with humans actively involved in all its variation, selection, and inheritance components.

Also, like biological evolution, the selective component of cultural evolution occurs on multiple levels at once. Various thoughts and behaviors compete for selection (attention and retention) within individual brains; individuals behaving differently compete for selection within their groups (tribes, sports teams, companies); groups behaving in diverse ways compete for selection within populations (associations, states, nations); and populations with different characteristics compete for selection (recognition, influence) within the human species around the globe.

Cooperative behavior evolved along with shared intentionality at the group level to empower humanity's greatest accomplishments. Over the course of evolutionary history, groups that learned how to cooperate and behave prosocially prevailed on the global stage over groups that were unable to suppress self-interested behavior at the expense of community concern.[3] Among many other benefits, the stability of cooperative, interdependent groups allows them to serve as building blocks for higher-level aggregations, such as towns grouping into counties, counties making up states, and states constituting a nation.

In specific contexts, such as matters of style or fashion, the idea that aspects of our culture evolve has been commonplace for a while. But the larger concept of cultural evolution of society as a whole is a complete non-starter in mainstream American political discourse because the very idea of human evolution by natural selection was correctly understood by most Christian religious leaders to be a direct threat to traditional dogma. As a result, recognition of biological evolution has been strongly resisted in education and political discussions since the 19th century.[4] Awareness of cultural evolution of society as a whole has been virtually non-existent. Notwithstanding this inhospitable climate, there are a few specific ways in which a widespread public understanding of cultural evolution could greatly benefit American political life:

- If we could come to see ourselves as collectively constructing culture as part of the dynamic of cultural evolution, we would want to assert our conscious intentionality into the process. Within this viewpoint, social engineering, policy changes, and new incentives are all means to the end of *purposive* or *guided* cultural evolution. Once you see yourself as an actor in the storyline of cultural evolution, you feel compelled to exercise whatever control you can over its destination.[5]

- The obvious way to guide cultural evolution is to harness existing political institutions to achieve desired ends. Thus, we could reframe politics from a battle to maintain existing levers of power into an inclusive, constructive debate over future goals and priorities. Instead of the same old ideological struggle, the narrative becomes "Today's status quo solutions worked and fit past conditions, but *conditions have evolved,* and *status quo solutions no longer work or fit present and future conditions.*" Politics could then become the forum to decide our country's future directions for ourselves through democratic deliberation; as it were, to design our own destiny.

- Moreover, cultural evolution can serve as a conceptual framework to help replace the entrenched economic growth regime with one of continuous improvement toward sustainability. The following section describes this approach.

Continuous Improvement Toward Sustainability

Under the established economic regime, steady (if not accelerating) growth is the standard of success expected for individual business entities and for the nation. A slower rate of growth is taken as a danger sign. If the national economy's growth rate slows down enough to worry the donor class, they expect the Federal government to adjust fiscal policy as needed to provide a corrective stimulus. In the standard economic paradigm, it is irrelevant that never-ending growth is intrinsically unsustainable. The central concern is to keep the economy growing. If there were to be sufficient political support for achieving sustainability and social justice goals—to the point of agreement to direct the economy toward those goals—there would remain the challenge of formulating a viable alternative to the economic growth imperative. My proposed alternative is the policy and practice of continuous improvement.

Continuous improvement and cultural evolution are kindred spirits. Both are dynamic systems that shape outcomes by retaining what works and fits, while discarding what does not. As described earlier (chapter nine), the essence of continuous improvement practice is a repeating feedback cycle consisting of (a) setting goals collectively, (b) implementing those goals, (c) gathering data to determine whether the goals are being met, (d) reviewing the feedback as a group, and (e) if and as needed, revisiting the goals, how to achieve them, and how to measure them.

My proposed economic policy has two fundamental objectives: (a) to replace an amplifying economic *growth* system with a stabilizing economic *social* system; and (b) to replace market-driven outcomes and values with ecological and humanity-driven outcomes and values. The two objectives are mutually necessary and supportive. In the old regime, an absence of regulatory constraints encourages the growth imperative; in the new regime, regulatory constraints representing non-market values provide boundary conditions to which businesses must adapt, putting the brakes on unlimited growth.[6] The linchpin of this kind of regulation regime are the values being measured— the indicators chosen to represent desired outcomes; to achieve broad buy-in and legitimacy, these and all the other value-laden choices in the system must be decided by inclusive democratic deliberation.

Decision makers will have no lack of indicator and measurement schemes to consider because socially concerned policymakers have been working for years (or decades) to develop them for both sustainability and social well-being outcomes.[7] Unfortunately, most of these metrics are structured to fit the conventional policy environment as alternatives to the Gross Domestic Product (GDP), the standard measure of national economic growth which tracks the total output of the U.S. economy for a fixed period. Alternative metrics may move the indicators toward sustainability—for example, by including outcomes like expenditures-on-renewable-energy or the ratio of expenditures on renewable versus fossil fuel energy as highly weighted factors—but the GDP index format and structure still measure the gross *size* of the economy, the growth system we aim to replace.

Such an exclusive focus on *output* measures is a crucial bottleneck. Including *input* indicators as well as output indicators allows a prospective index not only to measure economic size, but also to compare the effects of variable treatments (like "public spending on family benefits") on outputs. Better yet, an alternative Index can depart completely from the growth paradigm to better inform public policy. A case in point is The Social Wealth Economic Indicators system,[8] which uses existing international data sources to study the *relationships* between various "care investment" indicators (like "paid family work leave") and "human capacity" indicators (like "time spent on unpaid care work"). This kind of analysis directly identifies differential returns on social investments. Both sets of indicators include environmental as well as social welfare factors. A Social Wealth Index derived from these indicators is under development.[9]

The unregulated economic growth regime is harmful to both social and ecological systems, but not in the same way. We suffer from a *shortfall* of investment in funding the social foundation of human well-being, while at the same time we are *exceeding* the ecological ceiling of planetary system destabilization. The economist Kate Raworth created a striking image that combines both goals of our continuous improvement policy into what she calls "a radically new compass for guiding humanity this century," the Doughnut, as depicted in figure 11.1.

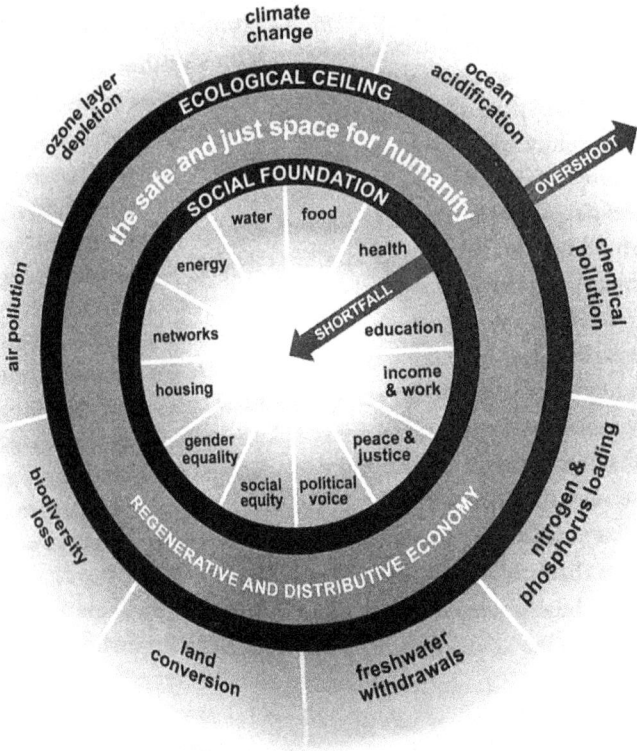

Figure 11.1 – The Doughnut
Adapted from Raworth (2017, p. 38)

In *Doughnut Economics*,[10] Raworth spells out the indicators for each of the elements in this diagram and uses an embellished version of the Doughnut to display the degree of shortfall and overshoot of each element.[11] This is precisely the "dashboard" logic of any graphic display that decision makers need to use to monitor continuous improvement feedback.

In practice, the choice of desired outcomes drives the political process, so the benefits of a continuous improvement policy will depend on how the political system interprets and implements the meanings of sustainability and social justice at any point in time. No doubt the first attempts will be relatively uniformed and insufficiently bold, but the strength of this approach is that feedback from early attempts necessarily leads to continuous improvement; and this process begets a virtuous cycle. As mentioned earlier, for the whole society to achieve sustainability, all industrial-era bureaucracies need to morph into more dynamic, adaptive systems. Turning the economic ship around is the most urgent instance of this general challenge, and it could and should serve as a model for all other organizations—at every level of government, military, and corporate enterprises—to learn to practice continuous improvement.

Democracy as Self-Government

To my mind, the concept of democracy as self-government is one of the three unimpeachable ideals humans have created. (The others are skeptical empiricism and the rule of law.) As discussed earlier, true self-government involves far more than periodic voting for representative public officials. Another benchmark is full equality under the law and in the culture. Equally important is citizen participation with agency—the ability to bring about meaningful results by their efforts. Full-bore democracy is not only a means of governance but also an end in itself. The self-determination and agency of self-governance bestow a unique intrinsic legitimacy to democracy. Only inclusive, truly democratic deliberation can claim legitimate authority for reconciling interests of individuals with the common good. With this image of self-government in sight, let us consider the kinds of changes it would take to undo key elements of the neoliberal regime and replace them with a vibrant democracy in America.

After four decades of domination, the neoliberal regime has harnessed the American political system to operate almost completely to benefit private and corporate interests over the public good. Besides favorable judicial appointments with long tenure, the toughest nut to crack is how donor money controls individual members of Congress, from funding their campaigns through lobbying for individual bills. This vise prevents passing legislation to change the rules that favor the regime. Legislative or constitutional reforms to reinvigorate democracy comprise at least three categories: (a) outlaw gerrymandering, reform or abolish the electoral college, and provide full representation for residents of the District of Columbia and Puerto Rico; (b) reject *Citizens United* and personhood for corporations, provide complete public funding for national elections, limit time allowed for campaigning, and dramatically reduce the scope of corporate lobbying; and (c) register everyone to vote automatically in national elections, use incentives and penalties to maximize turnout for elections, and seek to prohibit the specific techniques that states now use to make voting difficult. Any progress along these lines will make the achievement of other badly needed reforms that much more likely to succeed.

Great financial and social inequalities require significant proactive redistribution policies. On the financial side, familiar policies include progressive tax increases on personal income, capital gains, and corporate profits; a return to estate taxes, regulating financial industries, breaking up monopolies, and holding corporations liable for damage to public goods and resources. Another extremely beneficial policy would be to outlaw all derivative financial instruments lacking connection to real goods or services. Other options include increasing the minimum wage and the scope of unemployment insurance. But above and beyond such corrections to the massive transfer of wealth from lower-income to higher-income individuals and corporations over the past four decades, some systemic reconstruction of wealth ownership is needed to deflect America's march toward plutocracy. I will return to this topic in the next section, on democratic control of economic policy.

Existing inequalities in social capital and social justice often seem intractable, and certainly require significant proactive corrective policies. Social *capital* inequalities will be discussed shortly in the context of democratic control of economic policy. Social *justice* inequalities can seem the most intractable, baked as deeply as they are into America's history of slavery and ongoing white supremacy ideology and activism. Given the scope and depth of racism in America, I cannot imagine achieving social justice equality without also achieving most of the other institutional and policy changes contemplated in this chapter. That broader context includes reform of the electoral system to achieve true democracy at the polls, reform of Wall Street to dramatically reduce income inequality, empowering workers through democratic control of economic policy, reforming news and social media to serve the public interest, and greatly increasing public spending on universal health care (including mental health services), universal childcare, a robust public school system, and other public welfare needs.

Within this broader context, the entire social function of public safety needs to be reconceived from its present emphasis on coercion through lethal force and incarceration—with virtually no accountability—to a more humane conception of securing the community against antisocial behavior that persists despite all available support systems. A democratic society devoted to building solidarity would include institutions and policies that, over time, tend to decrease the intensity of hostile feelings between ethnic and racial groups. The history of integration of the U.S. Armed Forces is a good example of how a "mission-driven" organization can contribute to better racial relations (if not yet a semblance of justice for female soldiers).

Some version of mandated public service for all citizens, with no exceptions, can be designed to provide person power for important public needs while bringing together people from different life circumstances to "walk in each other's shoes." For such a policy to succeed, it must strike the right balance between matching personal interests to opportunities, on the incentive side, and ensuring that entitled people cannot game the system to defeat its communitarian objectives.

Media Accountability

Everything about democracy as self-government ultimately rests on well-educated and well-informed citizens. Those qualities are more essential than ever in the current century, in which information has become exponentially easier to disseminate on radio and television, and especially via online media unconstrained by either technological or legal limitations. The result has been a vast increase in the circulation of socially harmful misinformation, much of it deliberate, nefarious and illegal, and almost all of it purveyed or facilitated by profit-making US corporations. Those same companies use undisclosed and, in some cases, morally bankrupt techniques to manipulate viewing and buying habits and even control attention spans. Amid these harms, calls for media reform and regulation pose difficult questions about how to regulate speech in a democracy increasingly threatened by speech itself. A little history is of value in pondering that question.

The political fortunes of neoliberalism received a huge boost with the repeal of the Fairness Doctrine[12] in 1987, leading directly to the rise of politically-oriented talk radio during the 1990s, which featured conservative show hosts delivering strongly partisan polemics. Next came the ascendance of Fox News, a fiercely partisan conservative cable television network that had achieved the highest rating of any news channel by 2004 and has continued to lead the pack.[13] As Republican talking points became a litany of lies and conspiracy theories during the Trump administration, these media outlets amplified Trump's propaganda to many millions of listeners and viewers to the point of complicity in its real-world consequences.

Meanwhile the internet spawned social networks, of which Facebook is by far the most dominant. Over two billion people use Facebook every month, making the network's News Feed the most viewed and most influential aspect of the entire news industry.[14] Facebook's News Feed delivers content to each user according to algorithms designed to maintain the user's attention, notoriously relying on confirmation bias to effectively create "echo chambers," in which users see only content that reinforces their preconceptions. Of greatest importance, these algorithms do nothing to distinguish fact from fiction, or empirically based propositions from conspiracy theories. During the Trump administration, Facebook not only delivered heavy daily doses of lies and conspiracy theories to susceptible users but also served as a key platform by which white supremacist groups and other Trump supporters organized their collective activities.

The fact that news and social media greatly amplify lies and disinformation is a critical problem for democracy, but the deeper problem is the erosion of norms of reliable authority due to the lack of accountability in these domains. By regularly busting established norms, the Trump administration vividly demonstrated how much American institutions rely on them. Norms, in turn, depend upon repeated evidence that violations have consequences; in other words, accountability. What we witnessed in the Trump administration was an almost total breakdown in accountability on every level. As mentioned repeatedly in this book, transparency and accountability are the hallmarks of trust and legitimate authority.

Traditional broadcast media have long been subject to some degree of legal accountability. To operate at all, they have been required to seek and maintain government-issued licenses under laws requiring responsibility to the public. And they are subject to libel laws that punish publication of false information. Although those laws have not been adequately enforced, they establish the principle that media should be held accountable for what they push into the world. The exemption of Internet platforms from that principle is unrealistic and wrong and is now completely unmoored from its original purpose of shielding "infant" Internet companies from liability. We need policies that remove that exemption and provide media regulation based on democratic principles and values, not on the particular technology of dissemination.

Foremost among humanist democratic values is freedom of speech, so regulation of speech media must achieve a difficult and delicate balance between protecting that freedom while at the same time protecting the public from lies and falsehoods masquerading as truth. Achieving such a balance demands inclusive and intelligent democratic deliberation. To be effective, the results of this deliberation must hold platforms accountable for what they publish and provide rules and restrictions to clarify the boundaries of what is acceptable. Good starting points would be to expand the scope of media licensing and libel laws to all media and to reinstate some form of the Fairness Doctrine. More difficult but important questions include whether and how to require media to clearly distinguish entertainment from news, and news from opinion, and whether they should be required to re-establish a firewall between news and entertainment to insulate news from the profit motive, thus protecting citizens' rights to be well-informed with useful, factual journalism.

Education and Critical Thinking

To participate in self-government with agency, citizens require an education in *critical thinking*. Critical thinking is a toolbox of mental habits that can be developed at any age with appropriate guidance from parents, classroom teachers, friends, and mentors in any walk of life. Asking a young child to observe, describe, and "guess" something about a picture, object, or event is laying the foundation for all their future self-aware inferences. In teaching reading and literature, any interpretation of a story's meaning is grist for the mill of reflection about alternative interpretations and the reasons for one's choices. In mentoring an apprentice, every conversation is an opportunity to reflect on choices, alternatives, and reasons.

Clearly, one must already be a critical thinker to teach critical thinking. Ergo, public education for participative democracy will entail a massive increase in financial resources devoted to bringing the entire K-12 teaching profession up to speed, including heavy recruiting of new teachers, by raising all teacher salaries to competitive levels (contingent upon demonstrating the advanced capabilities required by critical-thinking teaching standards). In addition, the U.S. K-12 teaching profession must evolve toward continuous learning and improvement within the school building and regular work hours, as our most successful international competitors are already doing.

Another major component of the new education paradigm is strengthening the role of science education in a democratic society. To learn science at any level is to study the basic practice of posing a question, using systematic observation and data to answer the question, analyzing the data skeptically, and repeating the process as necessary. This practice is another example of critical thinking, the analog in the empirical world of interpreting the meaning of a story in the world of literature.

It is also another instance of continuous improvement. This view of science as the very "method of empiricism" reveals its simple and essential profundity and implies how pervasive science education should be throughout the curriculum. It follows that every subject, including "soft" ones like the arts and culture, can benefit from learning to frame empirical questions and to collect data systematically to evaluate answers. In no way is empirical inquiry limited to "objective" or "hard" data. Critical thinking is useful if not necessary in all walks of life.

Science is a social practice committed to skeptical empiricism, testability, coherence (sense-making), and fruitfulness. All humans recognize patterns and spin stories about them; the ones that count as science must be advanced in the spirit of the collective acquisition of useful knowledge. *To be scientific, claims must be testable and refutable in principle.* There is a "science" of cooking and a "science" of coding; these and many other practical sciences combine conceptual models with skills learned by experience. Science—as the method of empiricism— is learning by doing with the goal of continuous improvement. *Formal* science seeks to quantify or otherwise systematize knowledge that can be generalized, perhaps extrapolated, and hopefully be used to improve human well-being. In these ways the social practice of science exemplifies humanistic and democratic values.

Democratic Control of Economic Policy

Under America's neoliberal political regime of the last four decades, great wealth and political power have merged symbiotically into a virtual plutocracy ("a society ruled or controlled by people of great wealth or income"). In the previous section I listed familiar policy changes that could partly rectify income inequality extremes, but more than income inequality stands between the current regime and a vital democracy. Clear, structural constraints on property owners' rights are needed to overcome further inequalities in social and political capital. For example, the sanctioned exclusion of organized labor from the private sector effectively neuters workers' political clout. Another example, mentioned earlier, is how donor control of Congress prevents legislation to change rules favoring the wealthy.

The goal of democratic control of economic policy is to achieve lasting changes in established laws governing property ownership and other elements of economic policy that systematically favor "profit over people."[15] Specific policies will vary from one country to another and from time to time as circumstances dictate, but the principle of democratic control is a humanist moral imperative to maintain a bulwark against a political ideology committed to the *sanctity* of private property.

Imagine a new administration with a strong mandate to transform the American economy toward humanistic values. How might such an administration go about constructing a set of policies to submit to Congress? I will briefly describe the general outlines of two different approaches, both of which have great merit. Given the desirability of multiple perspectives, I would expect some synergistic blend of both approaches to fit the demands of a wide range of circumstances.

In *Agenda for a New Economy*,[16] the esteemed economist David Korten provides a compelling example of one approach, that of articulating a clear picture of an alternative to the status quo economic system and spelling out the steps needed to get from here to there. Korten provides a blistering critique of "Wall Street Capitalism" as creating "phantom" wealth (money disconnected from the production or possession of anything with real value), and contrasts this "Wall Street" with "Main Street," the world of local businesses and working people engaged in producing real goods and services to provide a livelihood for themselves, their families, and their communities. Within the broader context of a people-centered and sustainable future society, Korten's economic agenda includes: (a) measuring economic performance by indicators of health and well-being of people and the natural environment; (b) financial support for local and national food and energy independence; (c) returning manufacturing jobs to America; (d) building a sustainable national infrastructure; (e) rebalancing wealth distribution via universal health care, education, and other essential services; and via progressive taxation, as well as progressive wage and benefit rules; (f) a "true ownership society," with universal opportunity to own homes, and an ownership stake in enterprises on which one's livelihood depends; and (g) an extensive list of legislative proposals to reduce the power of Wall Street while reinvigorating the kind of local banking that effectively supports Main Street.[17]

The other approach is to leave specific economic policies to be determined by lawmakers, within an explicit political framework that proposes broad goals and various potential methods for achieving them. In the penultimate chapter of *Capital and Ideology*, the renowned French economist Thomas Piketty poses the questions, "What is a just society?" and "What is just ownership?" and then writes at length about the virtues of "transcend[ing] capitalism and private property and bring[ing] participatory socialism into being."[18] For purposes of this discussion, I take these to be his goals. To advance them, Piketty proposes to rely principally on the instruments of *legislation*, particularly as regards the balance of power between property owners and workers; and *progressive taxation* of property, inheritance, income, and carbon emissions. Among his proposals are forms of social ownership and shared voting rights in private firms; a universal capital endowment (a "system of public inheritance for all") to be given to each young adult (say at age 25), financed by a progressive tax on private wealth; transparency and a just distribution of all educational investments, including progressive taxes on private school endowments; writing fiscal justice into the Constitution; and "democratic equality vouchers" as a means to fund political parties and election campaigns. Piketty stresses that his proposals are "possible avenues of experimentation, not ready-made solutions."[19]

Whatever approach is taken, and whatever particular policies are enacted, the purpose of democratic control of economic policy is to provide truly equal opportunity for everyone to participate actively in the political and social life of the community; and for decisions about those policies, and the trade-offs between individual rights and the common good, to be made by the community as a whole. Thus, democracy as self-governance in its full expression becomes popular sovereignty, the power of ordinary people to make the decisions that matter.[20]

Global Governance for Sustainability

Despite the sincere and tireless efforts of thousands of climate activists and dedicated politicians and diplomats, the current international agreement to meet climate change goals—The Paris Agreement of 2016—is toothless and ineffectual. But even if the U.S., China, and India were to agree in principle to trilateral cooperation, there does not yet exist a governance structure that could hold these countries accountable to each other. The structure of the United Nations was created to make decisions in a nation-centric world. But intrinsically global problems cannot be solved by discretionary agreements among individual nations. Economic globalization of the last few decades has eroded the status of national borders in ways that only a global-level system can rectify.

The plain truth is: The unprecedented global climate crisis poses an existential threat to the entire human species, which requires the world's nations to create an unprecedented global governance system for the specific purpose of holding each other legally accountable to a mutually agreed plan of action for our collective survival. Nations urgently need to agree on a transparent and targeted cooperative regulatory scheme that is binding on all nations.

Something like this kind of global governance system is necessary now not only to monitor climate crisis commitments, but also to deal effectively with other unprecedented issues brought about by global interconnectedness. Among such global issues are public health (pandemics will continue), cybercrime (by states as well as private citizens), "surveillance capitalism"[21] (social media's extractive business models), and international migration and immigration to escape the horrors of climate change and domestic terrorism.

A radically new governance scenario may seem implausible after centuries of nation-centric competition on the global stage and four decades of neoliberal ideology, but a shift in worldview toward natural humanism could propel it into existence. Like it or not, we share a common fate on this one planet now. It is not only morally necessary to jump-start transparent global cooperation, but also, our very survival as a species depends on it!

This chapter has addressed the major dynamics of the neoliberal political regime that would have to be transformed to achieve the ideals of a natural humanist society. An economy addicted to expansion and controlled by political donors must be reconceived and restructured to protect the planet and to serve the public interest. A society verging on plutocracy must use legislation and progressive taxation to reconstruct itself as an inclusive, participatory democracy. I have applied the values and principles of natural humanism to offer strategies and policies toward these ends, not as presumptive solutions but as exemplary goals, possibilities to be considered, and suggestions for experimentation.

In advocating a natural humanist worldview, and in describing its practical implications, I am fully mindful of the great impediments to change. Indeed, in this book, I have spelled out the psychological and cultural underpinnings of those impediments, and the kinds of new thinking urgently required to overcome them. My goal has been to encourage and aid that new thinking, offering natural humanism as a valuable guide—a moral compass pointing toward humanity's survival and fulfillment. We humans make our cultures, and now, in the face of looming climate disaster, the cultures we make will determine our destiny on this planet. We are called to decide *Which Future?*

12
SUMMARY AND IMPLICATIONS

This book's objective is to present a natural humanist worldview, and to promote its merits as an alternative to the prevailing neoliberalism that threatens humanity's health and survival. The natural humanist worldview calls for critical paradigm shifts in our thinking as a species and, closer to home, in the traditional American mindset. This chapter concludes the book with a summing up in two ways. First, a table succinctly lays out the essential differences between the neoliberal and natural humanist worldviews. Second, I set forth the three basic tenets of natural humanism and their key implications.

Key Elements of Divergent Worldviews

The worldviews of neoliberalism and Natural Humanism are not merely different; they diverge profoundly. Natural humanism's "new vision" entails fundamentally new relationships of humanity with the planet and with each other. Instead of domination hierarchies fueled by individualism and private property, the core relationships of the new vision are interconnection and interdependence. The primary goals of sustainability and social justice are joined together not only in the practical sense that we cannot achieve one without the other, but also in the existential sense that both goals are rooted in relationships of interconnection and interdependence. These relationships are intrinsic properties of natural humanism, not derived from any central planning entity, like those that have failed so badly in the past.

Table 1, on the following pages, presents key elements of the two divergent worldviews, emphasizing how antithetical they are, and as a reminder of previously discussed topics and themes.

Table 1 – KEY ELEMENTS OF DIVERGENT WORLDVIEWS

	Neoliberal Political Regime (U.S.A. 1980-date)	Natural Humanism (subject of this book)
Climate and Sustainability	Earth belongs to humans. Ignore or deny climate change. The economy requires unlimited growth and consumption. Extract and burn fossil fuels. Profits trump a sustainable environment.	Human survival requires a healthy biosphere. Climate change is an urgent, existential threat. Use only renewable energy sources. Continuous improvement replaces quantitative growth goals. Define sustainability goals democratically and achieve them through monitored feedback. Global issues, including sustainability, require accountable global governance.
Role of government	Legislate lower taxes and minimal government services and regulations. Serve interests of banks, global corporations, and individuals as private investors and consumers.	Legislate optimal size government, regulations and taxes as needed to achieve social goals, including distributive fairness. Promote social justice, the common good, community, and participatory citizenship. Enforce constitutional and other civil rights.

Political economy	Promote and protect the sanctity of private property rights, unregulated markets, privatized public services (education, health care), and monetized personal information.	Democratic control of economic policy, including regulation in the public interest of: private ownership of public goods and personal information, markets and financial speculation, advertising and media.
Norms and Values	Individual self-interest, interpersonal competition, "tribal" loyalty, sanctity of beliefs and traditional authority. Economic libertarianism and fiscal social austerity.	Community concern, cooperation, mutual respect, caring, nurturance, interdependence, and solidarity. Fiscal social benevolence, as in a universally adequate standard of living.
Institutions and Policies	Domination hierarchies, coercive authority, and racial superiority. Militarized police and armed citizens. Great social inequalities of resources and of protection from harm.	Enhance human well-being, fulfillment, and social justice through egalitarianism and participatory democracy. Incentivize pluralism and diversity. Funding to promote public education, science, and critical thinking. Democracy as an end in itself.

Interpretation: The entries in this Table recapitulate topics and themes discussed in previous chapters. The Table does not stand on its own as a summary of the respective worldviews, which spring from different premises and beliefs about reality, causation, and the human condition and, as such, appeal to different sets of human emotions. These differences are addressed in this chapter's concluding section.

Three Main Tenets of Natural Humanism and Their Implications

This section spells out the main tenets (or "bottom-line values") of natural humanism *at the whole system level*. All the particular elements have been covered in previous chapters; the purpose here is to subsume and integrate these parts into the worldview as a whole. These three tenets should be read in conjunction with the preceding Divergent Worldviews table.

Tenet #1: Natural humanism begins with a rejection of any fixed human nature. In its place is the premise of an open-ended human condition.

Crucially, natural humanism begins with *a rejection of any fixed human nature*. Consistent with contemporary science, it posits instead a particular conception of the *human condition*: humans are born incomplete hybrids of *inherited* emotional/animal characteristics and *open-ended* mental capacities to be shaped into the language and belief systems of the child's native culture by caregivers/family and the local tribe/community. Beyond survival factors, we inherit *tendencies*, not necessities; and *we do not inherit culture, we create it for ourselves*.

We humans "live" in our belief systems, which are self-fulfilling; but *all belief systems are intrinsically limited and incomplete*. The three chapters of Part I develop and explore these ideas, including the pivotal role of *legitimate authority*. Legitimate authority bears the moral weight of replacing inevitability in a *pluralist* human condition. In a pluralistic world, the proper grounds for valid knowledge must incorporate multiple perspectives. It follows that diversity of viewpoints and being open to change are vital dispositions, and that democracy (as full self-governance) is the vital political process.

The change of mindset from neoliberalism to natural humanism entails a transformation from a pessimistic to an optimistic view of people's capacity to transform themselves. The lens of culture as a social construction opens up future possibilities unimaginable within the neoliberal frame. Cultural beliefs about human possibilities are self-fulfilling. Believing that people are selfish creates a society in which they increasingly behave that way. Believing in people's innate capacity and desire to care about others, and to further their own lives if given enough support to do so, is a necessary condition for these behaviors to predominate. If there is no presumptive right answer in a pluralistic world, the decisive social processes are deliberation, cooperation, and negotiation, not domination and coercion.

IMPLICATIONS: Our *human condition* allows for an open-ended plurality of cultures, norms, institutions, and beliefs; those we already have were invented by our predecessors, not given to them; and we are empowered to reinvent our belief systems any time we have the will to do so. Thus, how humans relate to the natural world and to each other is not fixed or inevitable; rather, it is always open to new possibilities, new inventions, and new results (covered in Part I).

In particular, the two demonstrably destructive and immoral linchpins of the neoliberal regime—domination hierarchies and economic man—are ripe for replacement by new, constructive, moral, and sustainable ways of living. We should do so, because we must act urgently to reduce the imminent danger from the global climate crisis threatening the very survival of our species (Part III).

> *Tenet #2: Natural humanism rejects and repudiates any presumption of native superiority (especially as) used to legitimate domination hierarchies.*

Authorities in support of domination hierarchies use presumptive supremacy to *legitimate* unequal, exploitive power and money regimes (chapters three, eight, and nine). Primary examples of domination hierarchies are (a) Earth belongs to humans (allowing rape and pillage of the atmosphere, water, and soil, and unlimited extraction and burning of nonrenewable fossil fuels); (b) colonialism and war over territory (justifying exploitation of indigenous populations and taking of property, even an entire nation); (c) slavery (enabling appropriation of populations as property, and human trafficking); and (d) racism and patriarchy (denying full citizenship and equal access to resources and opportunities based on race and gender). The effects of *human* domination are always taking, exploitation and destruction, whether of or from individuals, groups, or the whole environment.

Natural humanism rejects any presumption of native superiority (especially as) used to legitimate domination hierarchies. First, and most importantly, Earth does not belong to humans; humanity's fate has always been in the hands of Nature (chapter six). Second, humans genetically and existentially are all one species; alleged *superiority* is a discretionary cultural, not a fixed biological, relation (chapter eight). Third, *the actual order of* life on Earth consists of networks of interdependent ecologies, wherein hierarchies exist as means to limited ends in local contexts (chapter five). Consider the "rock-paper-scissors" game, which illustrates hierarchies in a circular system not unlike a typical ecosystem. Rock breaks scissors, scissors cut paper, and paper covers rock—a self-sufficient circular system in which each entity "dominates" and is "dominated" in turn.

Human domination systems are much too rarely based on such mutually constructive ecologies. They are almost always "one-way streets" in which benefits are reaped by the dominating at the expense of the dominated. In contrast, in biological nature, feedback flows both up and down interconnected control hierarchies (chapters five and nine). The human organizational equivalents are relationships of cooperation, reciprocity, and partnership, the natural and so much healthier alternatives to superiority and domination hierarchies.

IMPLICATIONS: Natural humanism rejects as illegitimate all forms of authority claimed or taken in the name of an alleged "natural order" or "higher power." There is simply no such order or power, no such source of legitimate authority, though lessons from the observed order of the natural world can and should inform the way humanity organizes itself. *Legitimate authority* requires transparent accountability and derives from collective decisions of free and willing followers to grant such power to a leader, position, or principle (chapter three). The ideal expression of legitimate authority is thus self-government, as manifested in an inclusive and egalitarian participative democracy (chapter ten).

Tenet #3: Natural humanism rejects the sanctity of private property rights that enable unconstrained exploitation of the environmental and social commons.

Under the neoliberal political regime, private property owners *acting lawfully* do not have to account for "externalities" on their balance sheets. In seeking profits, they need not account directly for their consequential destruction of the environmental or social commons. The most fundamental costs thus ignored, and borne by the public, are (a) the destructive climate effects of burning fossil fuels and (b) the denial of social justice from the domination of political power by private capital. Continual harm to and ultimate destruction of air, water, soil, and whole ecosystems, as well as harm to local communities, health care, journalism, privacy, and civil discourse, are just a few more examples of common goods and resources at the mercy of private investors, corporations, and speculators lawfully seeking greater (and usually short-term) profits from the exploitation of public resources.

In the neoliberal worldview (and the U.S. Constitution), the foregoing state of affairs is, to use a modern metaphor, "a feature, not a bug." The priorities and resulting defaults are intentional and fundamental. Government power is inherently constrained by law while merchant power is unconstrained by default. *The burden of proof is on the public* to justify constraints on the uses of private property and the pursuit of profits.

In contrast, natural humanism identifies the environmental and social commons as the source of life itself and of the principal prosocial values which must not be sacrificed for the sake of profit. Rather than "externalities," the environmental commons and the social commons are rightfully the bedrocks of society. The exploitation of privately-owned assets, *as it affects the commons*, must be subject to appropriate rules, determined on a case-by-case basis by inclusive, egalitarian democratic deliberation.

IMPLICATIONS: Humans cannot survive without healthy physical and social environments (chapters nine, ten); Earth's biosphere and humanity's social fabric belong to everyone, the common "property" of our species. No political or economic regime should allow excessive exploitation, much less destruction of these environments. Rights of private property owners may trump environmental commons or social commons interests only if an exception is granted explicitly by an inclusive democratic process on a case-by-case basis. By default, *the burden of proof is on private property owners* to justify "taking" from common resources without prior negotiated restitution and appropriate limitations.

Thus, *natural humanism "flips the script" of neoliberalism at its core.* Rather than build a political economy around the archetype of an individual profit-seeking "economic man," natural humanism embeds and interconnects all humans within the environmental and social commons that sustain and nourish them. Merchants and markets operate freely, but only within constraints determined through inclusive democratic deliberation. "Externalities" are thereby taken into account, and the healthy physical and social systems valued by natural humanism can be sustained.

In considering these three tenets, it is important to reflect upon the connections natural humanism makes among democracy, climate health and social justice. The first tenet reminds us that we live entirely in our self-created cultures—cultures we always have the power to choose and change. *If we have the will to do so*, we are free to determine our relationships to the rest of the natural world and to each other. We can choose to thrive on positive relationships fostering climate health, and political and economic arrangements that advance social justice.

With that freedom in mind, the second tenet sums up how those healthy relationships can and should be structured, with cooperation replacing domination and exploitation as the fundamental behavioral and organizational principle. In this tenet, we mirror biological nature, and understand that the health of our climate and our cultures rest on the same essential principles. Finally, the third tenet pinpoints the key economic and political implication of the cooperation principle, the ultimate humanistic priority of the "commons"—the natural and human resources we necessarily share and must preserve if there are to be climate health and social justice in our collective future.

Democracy is embedded in all three tenets. True pluralistic democracy recognizes our equality as humans, rejects domination and exploitation, and provides the means to make and to legitimate collective choices about the future of our life on this planet.

———————

In conclusion, the divergent worldviews of neoliberalism and natural humanism share all the characteristics of classic paradigm shifts. As explained in chapter two, no one is ever ready to abandon a worldview that makes sense of, and justifies the rightness of, what they believe to be normative and true. In the case of neoliberalism, the question is whether the existential urgency of the climate and social justice crises will ever be emotionally direct and powerful enough to overcome this resistance. The answer will depend on decisions made by thought and political leaders as they continue to respond to and frame the climate and social justice crises. While the future remains to be seen, this top-level summary should help readers better understand the essential core of the natural humanism paradigm, worldview, and moral philosophy.

ACKNOWLEDGMENTS

I am pleased to take this opportunity to acknowledge a handful of teachers, mentors, and places that stand out as formative influences on my path to writing *Which Future?*: Rachel Ferraro, my high school biology teacher, who taught me to think like a scientist; Gail Kennedy, the Amherst College philosophy professor who encouraged my lifetime proclivity to challenge basic assumptions; Barratt Junior High School in South Philadelphia, where I spent two pivotal years teaching mathematics to inner-city kids; Mark Lepper, my Stanford graduate supervisor, friend, and colleague, who taught me how to design experiments that meant something; and Marion "Mimi" Stearns, Center director at SRI International and mentor extraordinaire, from whom I learned how to do education policy research that mattered.

While working at SRI in 1979, I crossed paths with experts in the budding discipline of building scenarios, then called futurists. One report from this group described *The Emergent Paradigm: Changing Patterns of Thought and Belief*. Of all the dimensions of change discussed in the report, I was most captivated by the implications of the shift from objectivity to "perspectivity." Soon, I began to morph from a practicing, if skeptical, disciple of traditional science into an unaffiliated, cross-disciplinary independent scholar. While working for software development companies during the 1980s, I began to study a plethora of exciting new directions in science, philosophy, and politics on my own, selectively integrating the insights that made the most sense to me into my worldview.

Roughly thirty years ago, I made an initial attempt to consolidate my thinking into a book in the same vein as *Which Future?*, but never succeeded in creating a coherent narrative. In recent years, compelled by the intensifying ecological crisis, rampant social and economic inequalities, and, not incidentally, by further developments in the biological and social sciences that reinforced my confidence in what I had to say, I returned to thinking about how to create a coherent narrative. I took advantage of my close personal relationship with my old college roommate Jeremy Williams to elicit his feedback as I came up with potential book outlines. Jeremy's generative and supportive roles in *Which Future?* cannot be overstated. Nominally, he is the book's editor in the broadest, old-school sense of personal and critical support. He helped to shape the book's final structure, rode shotgun on every editorial decision, copy-edited every draft and revision, and provided moral support whenever I needed it. I literally could not have written the book without him.

I have relied on the kindness of many other friends and intellectual soulmates to bring *Which Future?* to fruition. I owe thanks to Mark Lepper, Sally Goldin, Rob Swezey, Joe Katz, Rosina Snow, Robert Ross, David Waldman, Jane David, Mike Greene, and Alan Mallach for reading and commenting on drafts of chapters. As experts in their respective fields, Mark Lepper and Rob Swezey contributed substantive improvements to Part I and Part II, respectively. Mark Lepper and Sally Goldin read the entire manuscript and helped enormously to improve its quality of expression. I bear full responsibility for whatever deficiencies persist.

Thanks also to Sally Goldin and Mike Greene for their assistance with post-manuscript publishing decisions. Jaya Chatterjee did the proofreading, Andy Meaden provided interior design for both print and ebook editions, and Cheryl Lenser compiled the index.

As the finale, I owe copious thanks and recognition to my spouse and life partner Jane David for her inestimable contributions to the *Which Future?* project. I have always been able to rely on all the ways a spouse can provide practical, tactical, and emotional support to an author, without which I would not have even considered jumping into the fire. But beyond that, Jane blends endless cheerleading with fearless critique, expressing her singular point of view in every conversation and every copy-edit into which she throws herself. I wouldn't have it any other way.

NOTES

Introduction

1   Walter Lippman, Public Opinion (New York: The Free Press, 1965, orig. 1922), p. 80

2   For well-contextualized, fact-based descriptions of the climate crisis, the following books are good sources: Naomi Klein, *This Changes Everything: Capitalism vs. The Climate* (New York: Simon & Schuster, 2014), Noam Chomsky and Robert Pollin, *Climate Crisis and the Global Green New Deal* (New York: Verso, 2020), and Bill McKibben, *Falter: Has the Human Game Begun to Play Itself Out?* (New York: Henry Holt, 2019)

3   The original report is accessible from https://www.ipcc.ch/sr15/. See https://www.nytimes.com/2018/10/09/opinion/climate-change-ipcc-report.html for *The New York Times* article summarizing its significance.

4   Others have written about ecology and social justice from a variety of perspectives; in particular, two books of historical interest are: Roy Morrison, Ecological Democracy (Boston, MA: South End Press, 1995) and Brian Morris, Pioneers of Ecological Humanism: Mumford, Dubos and Bookchin (Montreal, Canada: Black Rose Books, 2017). The former explains in practical and theoretical terms how to build an ecological democracy. The latter introduces readers to the Organic Humanism of Lewis Mumford, the Ecological humanism of René Dubos, and the Social Ecology of Murray Bookchin.

5   This term is used widely despite being contested and confusing.

It is lacking nuance and fails to convey the complexity of the schools of thought relevant to the political economy of the last four decades. I use it in this book because of its familiarity and widespread usage.

6   *This Changes Everything: Capitalism vs. The Climate* p. 462.

7   Beliefs about supernatural entities are formally a part of nature, but this fact in itself does not make them relevant to moral authority. I address this subject in chapter 3, "Belief Systems."

8   Walter Truett Anderson, *Reality Isn't What It Used to Be* (New York: Harper & Row, 1990) p. *xiii*.

9   Kindred writers on similar subjects are increasingly adopting a "biosocial" paradigm, which assumes a continuity of evolution from biology through culture through mind and an organic, dynamic human society. See, for example Riane Eisler and Douglas P. Fry, *Nurturing Our Humanity: How Domination and Partnership Shape Our Brains, Lives, and Future* (New York: Oxford University Press, 2019), David Sloan Wilson, *This View Of Life: Completing The Darwinian Revolution* (New York: Pantheon, 2019), and David C. Korten, *Agenda For A New Economy (2nd ed.)* (San Francisco: Barrett-Koehler, 2010).

10 I owe this language to a section called "Theory of Change" in Frederica Carugati and Margaret Levi, *A Moral Political Economy: Present, Past, Future* (Cambridge, UK: Cambridge University Press, 2021) p.7

Introduction to Part I: Human Reality Is Socially Constructed

1   Peter L. Berger and Thomas Luckmann, *The Social Construction of Reality: A Treatise in the Sociology of Knowledge* (New York: Doubleday & Company, 1966), p. 183.

Chapter One: Culture

1   Clifford Geertz, *The Interpretation of Cultures* (New York, Basic Books, 1973), p. 49.

2   According to Wikipedia, the conventional definition of
     culture is "the social behavior and norms found in all human
     societies." Thus, culture includes both material (such as
     technology, architecture, and art) and immaterial aspects (such
     as mythology, philosophy, literature, and science); the customs,
     traditions, and values of an ethnic group or nation; and the
     set of knowledge acquired over time. Instead, the topic of this
     chapter is culture (unconventionally) defined as the "fabric
     of meaning in terms of which human beings interpret their
     experience and guide their actions" (Geertz, *Interpretation,* p.
     145); thus defined, culture is the *meaning* of all the conventional
     entities listed in Wikipedia, as well as the symbolic medium in
     which self and identity develop.

3   Terrence W. Deacon, *The Symbolic Species: The Co-evolution of
     Language and the Brain* (New York: W.W. Norton, 1997), pp.
     43-46. Actually, the whole book is devoted to the argument. See
     also the conclusion to John R. Searle, *The Construction of Social
     Reality* (New York: The Free Press, 1995), p. 228.

4   "There are no gods in the universe, no nations, no money, no
     human rights, no laws, and no justice outside the common
     imagination of human beings." Yuval Noah Harari, *Sapiens: A
     Brief History of Humankind* (New York: HarperCollins, 2015)

5   As individual organisms, humans are not comparable to ants,
     lichens, forests, and other networked superorganisms wherein
     intentionality is beside the point and unnecessary to achieve
     their goals.

6   Michael Tomasello, *Becoming Human: A Theory of Ontogeny*
     (Cambridge, MA: Harvard University Press, 2019). See also
     Searle, *Social Reality*, p. 228, "What is special about culture is
     the manifestation of collective intentionality…"

7   Jerome Bruner, *Acts of Meaning* (Cambridge, MA: Harvard
     University Press, 1990), p. 67-97.

8   Geertz, *Interpretation*, p. 49.

9   Alan Page Fiske, Shinobu Kitayama, Hazel Rose Markus, and
     Richard E. Nisbett, "The Cultural Matrix of Social Psychology,"

in D. Gilbert, S. Fiske, & G. Lindzey, *The Handbook of Social Psychology, Vol. 2* (4th ed., pp. 915-981) (San Francisco: McGraw-Hill, 1998). On this point see especially pp. 916-919 on "the mutual constitution of culture and the psyche."

10   Bruner, *Meaning*, p. 11.

11   Richard E. Nisbett, Kaiping Peng, Incheol Choi, and Ara Norenzayan, "Culture and Systems of Thought: Holistic Versus Analytic Cognition," *Psychological Review* 108(2) (2001), 291-310.

12   In general, culture is the world as studied through the lens of anthropology while social structure is the same world as studied through the lens of sociology. At best, psychologists span these two perspectives. This chapter in particular attempts to integrate all three perspectives.

13   Fiske et al., "Cultural Matrix," pp. 919-926.

14   Geert Hofstede, Gert Jan Hofstede, and Michael Minkov, *Cultures and Organizations: Software of the Mind, Revised and Expanded Third Edition* (New York: McGraw-Hill, 2010)

Chapter Two: Sense Making

1   The concept of the brain as a predictive system is developed in chapter 5 of Jeff Hawkins with Sandra Blakeslee, *On Intelligence* (New York: Henry Holt, 2004), pp. 85-105.

2   Thomas Gilovich and Lee Ross, *The Wisest One in the Room: How You Can Benefit from Social Psychology's Most Powerful Insights* (New York: Free Press, 2015), pp. 13-41.

3   Daniel Kahneman, *Thinking, Fast and Slow* (New York: Penguin Books, 2011). Kahneman uses "System 1" and "System 2" to refer to what I call "intuition" and "rationality."

4   Countless neuroscience books explain the fundamentals of how the brain works. I rely primarily on those by Antonio Damasio, especially *Self Comes to Mind: Constructing the Conscious Brain* (New York: Random House, 2010). For a compact and entertaining primer, I recommend the Appendix titled "Neuroscience 101" to Robert M. Sapolsky, *Behave: The Biology*

of Humans at Our Best and Worst (New York: Penguin Books, 2017).

5   The single most important and influential article on this subject is Amos Tversky and Daniel Kahneman, "Judgment under uncertainty: Heuristics and biases," *Science* 185 (1974), 1124-1131. To dig deeper, the best compendium is Daniel Kahneman, Paul Slovic, and Amos Tversky (Eds.), *Judgment under uncertainty: Heuristics and biases* (New York: Cambridge University Press, 1982).

6   Leon Festinger, *The Theory of Cognitive Dissonance* (Stanford, CA: Stanford University Press, 1957)

7   Daniel Goleman, *Vital Lies, Simple Truths: The Psychology of Self-Deception* (New York: Simon and Schuster, 1986), pp. 121-123.

8   Irvin Janis, *Victims of Groupthink* (Boston: Houghton Mifflin, 1972)

9   Matthew T. Gailliot et al., "Self-control relies on glucose as a limited energy source: willpower is more than a metaphor." *Journal of Personality and Social Psychology.* 92:325-36 (2007) and Matthew T. Gailliot and Roy F. Baumeister, "The physiology of willpower: linking blood glucose to self-control." *Personality and Social Psychology Review.* 11:303-27 (2007)

10   I want to acknowledge the primacy of emotion from an evolutionary perspective, but it would take this topic too far afield to discuss it here.

11   Gender identity is the exception that proves the rule, being primarily under biological control.

12   Bruner, *Meaning*, p. 22, referencing Charles Taylor from his book, *Sources of the Self.*

13   This usage of the term "paradigm" originated in 1962 with Thomas S. Kuhn, *The Structure of Scientific Revolutions, Second Edition, Enlarged* (Chicago: University of Chicago Press, 1970) (first edition 1962). In the six decades since then, the concept has been widely accepted, adopted, and expanded way beyond Kuhn's original conception.

14   My "paradigm" concept draws on the social paradigm notion in Fritjof Capra and David Steindl-Rast with Thomas Matus, *Belonging to the Universe* (New York: HarperCollins, 1991), p. 34.

15   To clarify a potential source of confusion, let me distinguish the current discussion of "perspective, vision, or view of reality" in paradigms from earlier discussions of "perspective" in the context of pluralism. At issue in pluralism is the *diversity* of individual and cultural perspectives in making sense of the vastness and complexity of reality. I emphasized the inherent *selectivity* (incompleteness) of each perspective to argue the need for pluralism, to combine multiple perspectives in order to achieve a full picture. In the context of paradigms, however, a relatively *homogeneous* community of practice shares a singular perspective, vision, or view of reality, which helps bind the group together around other shared commitments. The inherent selectivity (incompleteness) of a given paradigm becomes an issue for the group only when the paradigm is challenged.

16   J. T. Fraser, *Of Time, Passion, and Knowledge: Reflections on the Strategy of Existence, Second Edition* (Princeton, N.J.: Princeton University Press, 1990) (first edition 1975), p. 160.

17   Sally E. Goldin suggested this example in a *personal communication*.

18   Searle, *Social Reality*, pp. 34-35.

Chapter Three: Belief Systems

1   Peter L. Berger and Thomas Luckmann, *The Social Construction of Reality: A Treatise in the Sociology of Knowledge* (New York: Doubleday & Company, 1966), p. 110.

2   Jonathan Haidt, *The Righteous Mind: Why Good People are Divided by Politics and Religion* (New York: Random House, 2012). This point is a premise of Haidt's book. Also, I know of at least one religion whose followers know themselves as "the chosen people." I assume other religions get the same point across one way or another.

3   Goleman, *Vital Lies*.

4   Haidt, *Righteous Mind*, and especially Hugo Mercier and
      Dan Sperber, *The Enigma of Reason: A New Theory of Human
      Understanding* (New York: Penguin Books, 2018)

5   Michael Polanyi, *The Study of Man* (Chicago: University of
      Chicago Press, 1959), pp. 11-39.

6   Gilovich and Ross, *Wisest*, pp. 2-4.

7   Sally E. Goldin, personal communication.

8   See also Michele Gelfand, *Rule Makers, Rule Breakers: How
      Tight and Loose Cultures Wire Our World* (New York: Scribner,
      2018) for wonderful and illuminating stories of the history and
      circumstances of many specific cultures and cultural patterns.

9   *Webster's Ninth New Collegiate Dictionary* (Merriam-Webster,
      1984), s.v. "authority."

10   Herbert A. Simon, *Administrative Behavior, Second Edition*
      (New York: Macmillan, 1961), pp. 125-134.

11   Raymond Aron, *Main Currents of Sociological Thought II:
      Durkheim, Pareto, Weber* (New York: Doubleday & Company,
      1967)

12   George Lakoff and Mark Johnson, *Philosophy in the Flesh: The
      Embodied Mind and Its Challenge to Western Thought* (New
      York: Basic Books, 1999), pp. 301-320. An in-depth discussion
      of the metaphorical basis of moral authority and two versions of
      parental authority.

13   Quakers, especially Universalists, reject the notion of external
      authority. See, for example https://transitionquaker.blogspot.
      com/2014/02/authority-and-leadership.html

14   John Dewey, *The Quest for Certainty* (New York, Minton, Balch
      and Co., 1929)

15   Gelfand, *Rule Makers*, p.224.

16   Heinz R. Pagels, *The Dreams of Reason* (New York: Simon and
      Schuster, 1988), p. 328.

17   *Ibid.*

18   *Ibid.* See also Mark Johnson, *Morality for Humans: Ethical
      Understanding from the Perspective of Cognitive Science*

(Chicago: University of Chicago Press, 2014) pp. 163-191.
Johnson argues from the perspective of cognitive science that
"the greatest sin of moral philosophy is moral fundamentalism."

19 Johnson, *Morality*, p. 14 goes even further, arguing that the
    quest for transcendental foundations could never be successful
    given the limitations of human understanding.

20 Many progressive religious organizations are dedicated to
    stretching the boundaries of traditional dogma, and otherwise
    creating vital communities far removed from absolute authority.
    I applaud them all and take them as the "exceptions that prove
    the rule."

21 Anderson, Reality, p. *xiii.*

Introduction to Part II: Humanity In Nature

1 Carlo Rovelli, *Helgoland: Making Sense of the Quantum
   Revolution* (New York: Riverhead Books, 2021), p. 203.

2 Earth is distinctive: from a distance a few other planets appear
   similar in surface features to the earth, but the earth is where
   homo sapiens evolved and the only place known to sustain life.

Chapter Four: Systems Thinking

1 Arthur Koestler, *The Ghost in the Machine* (London:
   Hutchinson, 1967) is credited with the concept and explication.

2 Ervin Laszlo, *A Strategy for the Future: The Systems Approach to
   World Order* (New York: George Braziller, 1974), p. 32.

3 Donella Meadows, "Whole Earth Models and Systems," *Co-
   Evolution Quarterly* (Summer 1982), 98-108

4 Although sometimes the whole is just *different* from the sum
   of its parts. A commonplace example is hydrogen and oxygen
   combining into water: the whole has totally different properties
   from its constituent parts. Cf. Peter Corning, *Synergistic
   Selection: How Cooperation Has Shaped Evolution and the Rise
   of Humankind* (Hackensack, N.J.: World Scientific, 2018), p.12.

5 This example appears in Peter M. Senge, *The Fifth Discipline:*

The Art and Practice of The Learning Organization (New York: Doubleday, 1990), pp. 73-79, who credits his entire chapter to the inspiration of the Meadows, *Co-Evolution* article.

6   The one other *basic* element in many feedback processes is a delay (any interruption in the flow of influence that slows down its consequences). In practice, in complex systems at all levels from micro-organisms to the biosphere, combinations of reinforcing and balancing feedback processes, including delays, are interconnected in multiple ways.

7   Gregory Bateson, *Mind and Nature: A Necessary Unity* (New York: Dutton, 1979); current edition (Cresskill, N.J.: Hampton Press, 2002)

Chapter Five: Living Systems

1   Terrence W. Deacon, *Incomplete Nature: How Mind Emerged from Matter* (New York: W.W. Norton, 2012), p. 274.

2   Some nonliving things have some properties of living things, such as crystals that self-organize, and perhaps some Artificial Intelligence algorithms, so the distinction is not absolute.

3   Fritjof Capra and Pier Luigi Luisi, *The Systems View of Life: A Unifying Vision* (New York: Cambridge University Press, 2014), p. 132.

4   To clarify: nervous systems as a whole are *structurally* closed, while the cellular constituent parts (neurons) of nervous systems are open energy systems.

5   Genetic instructions are constituted as a network of information that may be altered throughout the lifetime of organisms as a result of life experiences. More on this topic later in the chapter.

6   Damasio, *Self*, p. 45.

7   Physicist and systems engineer William T. Powers [William T. Powers, *Behavior: The Control of Perception* (Chicago: Aldine Publishing, 1973) and William T. Powers, *Living Control Systems* (Gravel Switch, KY: The Control Systems

Group, 1989)] hypothesized that the underlying, elemental mechanism of all adaptation *within an organism* is the control system. He argues as follows: Control systems change output (behavior or otherwise) when they sense a deviation from the reference value they are controlling; organisms adapt to changes internally or externally by doing something different until the action restores the reference level.

8   Humberto R. Maturana and Francisco J. Varela, *The Tree of Knowledge: The Biological Roots of Human Understanding* (Boston: Shambhala Publications, 1992)

9   Deacon, *Incomplete*, p. 175.

10   John H. Holland, *Adaptation in Natural and Artificial Systems* (Cambridge, MA: M.I.T. Press, 1992), p. 197. (First edition, University of Michigan, 1975)

11   I use the term "development" here in reference to single cell organisms more loosely than some biologists would.

12   The essential difference between physics and biology is the non-deterministic, process-oriented, circular model of causation that characterizes living systems. As previously discussed, everything biological must obey the laws of physics—biology is constrained by them—and deterministic causation sufficiently explains the mechanical components of living systems. However, determinism is *necessary but not sufficient* to adequately explain living systems.

13   Eva Jablonka and Marion J. Lamb, *Evolution in Four Dimensions: Genetic, Epigenetic, Behavioral, and Symbolic Variation in the History of Life, revised edition* (Cambridge, MA: M.I.T. Press, 2014). The main new concept is that variation in an organism's phenotype is the result not only of mutations (as the "gene-centric" paradigm assumes), but also, and more importantly, of epigenetic, behavioral, and symbolic factors. Epigenetic changes occur at the cellular level. For example, all organs in the body have the same DNA; what distinguishes liver cells from stomach cells is which subsets of genes were switched on and off very early in development. Similarly,

differences in diet, stress, exercise, and exposure to toxins in later development result in different genes being switched on or off. These are examples of epigenetic factors. Behavioral factors include birds' changing nesting habits because of environmental changes and primates' social learning of new ways to find food. Symbolic factors are changes in language and culture that affect how each generation differs from the previous one.

14   In common-sense psychology human intentionality typically connotes consciousness, but that puts the cart before the horse; we are often conscious of our intentions, but awareness is not necessary for behavior to be goal-directed or purposive. As discussed in chapter two, most anticipation and purposive action is initiated intuitively, without conscious awareness.

15   Each class of living things embodies its own unique structure, and has the goal of maintaining that particular structure, so this structure (in its detailed specifics) is the logically antecedent "cause" of the organism's behavior. Note here that causation is located *inside*, not outside the organism. Of course, organisms act in response to events *outside* them. But those events do not "cause" the response. Rather, according to William T. Powers' Perceptual Control Theory, external events trigger internal systems of comparators, which compare the *perception* of the event to an internal reference of the expected or desired perception. The discrepancy dictates some action to reduce it. In explaining his theory, Powers illustrates the core idea with the example of steering a car. If the goal is to keep the car going straight in the middle of the road, the actions needed to do this are determined by what the driver perceives as deviations from center. These cannot be predicted in advance, nor can they be explained in stimulus-response terms. Instead, whatever happens in the driver's visual field will be passed on as signals to lower control systems that will make appropriate corrections.

16   Damasio, *Self*, p. 49.

17   Mitsuru Shimizu and Brett W. Pelham, "Postponing a date with the Grim Reaper: Ceremonial events and mortality," *Basic and Applied Social Psychology*. 30 (1): 36–45 (2008)

18   The exception that proves the rule is hydrothermal vent ecosystems in the ocean's depths, where the energy source is chemicals, not photons.

19   Fritjof Capra, *The Web of Life: A New Scientific Understanding of Living Systems* (New York: Anchor Books, 1996), p. 178.

20   Capra and Luisi, *Systems View*, p. 344.

21   This estimate assumes that consumption per person continues at the same rate. It will be interesting to see how the carrying capacity concept evolves as humans continue to fill the oceans with plastics that do not degrade.

22   Capra, *Web of Life*, p. 106.

23   James Lovelock, *Healing Gaia* (New York: Harmony Books, 1991)

24   Capra and Luisi, *Systems View*, p. 349.

Chapter Six: Humanity's Relationship to Nature

1   As exemplified by the classic injunction of Genesis 1:28 to "Be fruitful and multiply and fill the earth and subdue it, and have dominion over the fish of the sea and over the birds of the heavens, and over every living thing that moves on the earth." *The English Standard Version Bible (New York: Oxford University Press, 2009)*

2   *This Changes Everything: Capitalism vs. The Climate*, p. 285.

3   Donella H. Meadows, Dennis L. Meadows, and Jørgen Randers, *Beyond The Limits: Confronting Global Collapse, Envisioning a Sustainable Future* (Post Mills, VT: Chelsea Green, 1992)

4   Of course, this issue is not unique to America; most of the industrialized world, regardless of region or political or economic system, is also part of the problem.

5   This is precisely the reason many religious leaders have always tried to keep teaching about evolution out of local schools.

Chapter Seven: Life's Healthy Operating Principles

1   Benyus, *Biomimicry*, p. 9.

2   Peter Corning, *Synergistic Selection: How Cooperation Has Shaped Evolution and the Rise of Humankind* (Hackensack, N.J.: World Scientific, 2018)

3   The exception that proves the rule is hydrothermal vent ecosystems in the ocean's depths, where the energy source is chemicals, not photons. [this is a repeat of endnote 18, chapter 5]

4   Benyus, *Biomimicry*, p. 260-263 provides good examples of efficient energy uses.

5   Naomi Klein describes this situation eloquently in *This Changes Everything*, p. 285.

6   Hofstede et al., *Cultures and Organizations*, p. 95.

Part III Introduction: Natural Humanism

1   Eisler, *Chalice and Blade*, p. 195.

Chapter Eight: Natural Morality

1   Both morality and ethics pertain to the normative part of social philosophy, the evaluation of what's good or bad and what's right or wrong. The terms "morality" and "ethics" are usually defined in reference to each other, as I discovered in looking them both up. Morality seems to have the more general connotation and usage, while ethics more often refers to rules or guidelines within a particular profession or institutional context (as in, What are the ethical boundaries on gene-splicing research?). Moral issues are the broad, global questions; ethical issues are which path to take in *this* case. The term morality seems to fit my purposes better.

2   As documented most thoroughly and engagingly in a series of books by the esteemed primatologist Frans de Waal. The one I have relied on most for this section is *The Bonobo and the*

Atheist: In Search of Humanism Among the Primates (New York: W. W. Norton, 2013)

3   Damasio, *Self*, chapter two ("From Life Regulation to Biological Value") offers a compelling interpretation of this topic.

4   De Waal, *Bonobo*, p. 234.

5   De Waal, *Bonobo*, p. 160.

6   Especially noteworthy in this regard are Buddhist teachings to the point that the causes of suffering are universal among humans.

7   See Robert B. Reich, *The Common Good* (New York: Alfred A. Knopf, 2018) and Michael J. Sandel, *The Tyranny of Merit: Can We Find the Common Good?* (New York: Farrar, Straus and Giroux, 2020) for excellent analyses of the concept.

8   Eisler and Fry, *Nurturing Our Humanity* is a deep and penetrating study of domination and partnership that resonates strongly with natural humanism on many levels.

9   George Lakoff and Mark Johnson, *Philosophy in the Flesh: The Embodied Mind and Its Challenge to Western Thought* (New York: Basic Books, 1999), p. 304 uses the word "repugnant" in this context. I loved the word choice and want to acknowledge the source.

10   Sapolsky, *Behave*, p. 107.

11   One relevant framework for understanding this dynamic is that of Isabel Wilkerson, *Caste: The Origins of Our Discontents* (New York: Random House, 2020)

12   D. S. Wilson, *This View of Life*, pp. 90-91.

13   For example, as in Alexis de Tocqueville, *Democracy in America*, trans. George Lawrence, ed. J.P. Mayer (New York: Doubleday, Anchor Books, 1969), originally published in two volumes, 1835 and 1840.

14   2019 Commonwealth Fund International Health Policy Survey of Primary Care Physicians accessed from https://www.commonwealthfund.org/publications/surveys/2019/dec/2019-commonwealth-fund-international-health-policy-survey-

primary on October 30, 2021.

15	Figure 2.4.1b, "Pre-tax incomes of the Top 1% and Bottom 50% in the US, 1962-2014" from the *World Inequality Report 2018* accessed from https://wir2018.wid.world/contents.html on October 30, 2021.

16	The early months of the COVID-19 pandemic provided a striking example of Americans' extreme individualism resulting in painfully obvious and morally unforgivable consequences for the nation. As of mid-June 2020, there was still an opportunity to level off the rate of new cases of the novel coronavirus, if only the vast majority of Americans would continue to follow public health directives to "social distance" and wear face coverings in public. Absent strong leadership, however, most young adults did not take the "social distance" directive seriously. And Donald Trump had already begun to politicize the "choice" to wear face masks, prompting a sizeable minority of individuals to forego wearing them while justifying that action as an individual choice (thereby encouraging others to do the same). As if on cue, the rate of new COVID-19 infections began to increase dramatically, spreading from the very locations where people prominently ignored public health directives. On June 15, the CDC nationwide seven-day moving average of new COVID-19 cases per day was 21,132, having steadily drifted down from its previous high of 31,994 on April 12. By July 24, a mere five weeks later, the national average of new cases per day reached a peak of 66,960. [*CDC webpage*] This was a clear case of individual actions directly undermining a critical, nationwide public health behavioral program because those individuals proudly chose to indulge self-interest at the expense of community concern.

17	A few notable examples are Klein, *This Changes Everything*, Korten, *Agenda for a New Economy*, Carugati and Levi, *A Moral Political Economy*, Anthony Biglan, *Rebooting Capitalism* (Eugene, OR: Values to Action, 2020), Kate Raworth, *Doughnut Economics* (White River Junction, VT: Chelsea Green, 2017), and Thomas Piketty, *Capitalism and Ideology* (Cambridge, MA: Belknap/Harvard University Press, 2020)

Chapter Nine: Life's Lessons For Sustainability

1   The best place to start is with Lester R. Brown, *Plan B 3.0: Mobilizing to Save Civilization* (New York: W.W. Norton, 2008)

2   Many people—religious and secular alike—attribute life to Gaia, are absorbed in planetary consciousness, or believe in other forms of Deep Ecology. Perhaps the best book in this vein is Edward Goldsmith, *The Way: An Ecological World-view* (Boston, MA: Shambhala, 1993). Furthermore, many relationships of indigenous cultures to nature are infused with spirituality. And Pope Francis wrote a magnificent Encyclical Letter, *On Care for Our Common Home*, which delves deeply into the ecological crisis and its moral implications from the perspective of the Catholic Church: Francis, *Encyclical Letter "Laudato Si'" (Praise Be To You): On Care for Our Common Home* (Our Sunday Visitor, 2015).

3   See Brown, *Plan B* for a comprehensive summary of what we need to do.

4   Eisler and Fry, *Nurturing Our Humanity* makes the case with striking authority.

5   Especially pertinent to understanding the interconnectedness of everything is the concept of "Interbeing," first articulated by the late Thich Nhat Hanh, the world's most influential Buddhist teacher. See Thich Nhat Hanh, "What is Interbeing? excerpt from Meena Srinivasan, *Teach Breathe Learn* accessed 11/2/2021 from http://www.rinagpatel.com/blog/2016/9/2/what-is-interbeing-by-thich-nhat-hanh

6   I do not recall where I read this specific point, but the larger issue of the difficulty of modeling Earth's carrying capacity is well documented here: Safa Motesharrei and nineteen others, "Modeling sustainability: population, inequality, consumption, and bidirectional coupling of the Earth and Human Systems," *National Science Review*, Volume 3, Issue 4, December 2016, pp. 470-494 accessed 11/2/2021 from https://academic.oup.com/nsr/article/3/4/470/2669331

7   Senge, *The Fifth Discipline*.

8   Michael Walzer, *Spheres of Justice: A Defense of Pluralism and Equality* (New York: Basic Books, 1983)

9   In particular, so-called "learning algorithms" do not learn how to learn; they learn how to extract patterns from data according to the objectives of their human designer. That they may do this better than a human could is only putting unrivaled power in the hands of those who design the algorithm. Thus, AI is a dangerous technology because of the unprecedented control it gives to those who design algorithms.

10 As strongly advocated by David Korten in *Agenda For A New Economy.*

Chapter Ten: Humanist Values And Principles

1   Al Gore, *Earth in the Balance: Ecology and the Human Spirit* (New York: Houghton Mifflin, 1992), p. 366, crediting Erik H. Erikson: "As Erikson once wrote," …

2   Thomas Piketty, *Capitalism and Ideology* (Cambridge, MA: Belknap/Harvard University Press, 2020)

3   Abraham Maslow, *Motivation and Personality* (New York: Harper & Brothers, 1954), Chapter Four.

4   Maslow's two higher levels are "The Esteem Needs" and "The Need for Self-Actualization." These levels are fundamental to Maslow's theoretical contributions to humanistic psychology, but their definitions are so bound to culture rather than biology that they do not belong in my conception of basic needs.

5   Maslow, *Motivation*, pp. 41-42.

6   Ian Gough, *Heat, Greed, and Human Need: Climate Change, Capitalism and Sustainable Wellbeing* (Cheltenham, UK: Edward Elgar, 2017). Gough's "Theory of Human Need" dovetails across the board with my views in this chapter.

7   Joan C. Tronto, *Who Cares?* (Ithaca, NY: Cornell University Press, 2015), p.4.

8   Anthony Biglan, *The Nurture Effect* (Oakland, CA: New Harbinger, 2015), p. 196.

9   Ibid.

10 Ibid., p. 204.

11 "Building Universal Family Care." Special issue, *The American Prospect*, 31, no. 6 (2020).

12 *Universal Declaration of Human Rights, Illustrated Edition* (New York: The United Nations, 2015) Accessed from https://www.un.org/en/udhrbook/pdf/udhr_booklet_en_web.pdf, p. 52.

13 Jaak Panksepp, *Affective Neuroscience: The Foundations of Human and Animal Emotions* (New York: Oxford University Press, 1998), pp. 53 & 223.

14 Edward L. Deci and Richard M. Ryan, *Intrinsic Motivation and Self-Determination in Human Behavior* (New York: Plenum Press, 1985)

15 Anne Case and Angus Deaton, *Deaths of Despair and the Future of Capitalism* (Princeton, NJ: Princeton University Press, 2020)

16 Deci and Ryan, *Intrinsic Motivation*.

17 Albert Bandura, *Self-efficacy: The Exercise of Control* (New York: Freeman, 1997)

18 My personal bête noire is a group of business practices that feel predatory. One is targeted advertising that follows me around the internet the minute I search for a particular product or service. Another is the algorithmic selection of news feeds based on user profiles. Last is the "autostart" of videos on web pages or streaming video sites. In each case the service provider has decided that greater profit outweighs my desire to be left alone to make a decision for myself. Business practices thwarting my autonomy and self-determination always upset me. I wish there were a principled way to identify a common feature of them that could be outlawed legislatively.

Chapter Eleven: Toward A Natural Humanist Society

1   Dewey, *Human Nature*, pp. 21-22.

2   See D. S. Wilson, *This View of Life*, and Jablonka and Lamb, *Evolution in Four Dimensions*, chapter six and part III.

3   D. S. Wilson, *This View of Life* includes an excellent exposition of this topic.

4   It has been a long, uphill battle for educators in many states to be allowed to teach evolution in public schools.

5   David Sloan Wilson, Steven C. Hayes, Anthony Biglan, and Dennis D. Embry, "Evolving the Future: Toward a Science of Intentional Change." *Behavioral and Brain Sciences* 37(4) 395-460.

6   In biology, of course, a lack of control on growth is the cause of cancer.

7   Gough, *Heat, Greed and Human Need*, p. 71 lists four of them: the Index of Sustainable Welfare, the Genuine Progress Indicator, the Genuine Savings Indicator, and the System of Environmental Economic Accounting.

8   Indradeep Ghosh with Riane Eisler, *Social Wealth Economic Indicators: A New System for Evaluating Economic Prosperity* (Center for Partnership Studies, 2014) Accessed 2//17/2021 from https://centerforpartnership.org/programs/caring-economy/indicators/

9   Center for Partnership Studies, *The Social Wealth Index* (under development, 2021) Accessed 2/17/2021 from https://centerforpartnership.org/programs/caring-economy/social-wealth-index/

10 Kate Raworth, *Doughnut Economics: 7 Ways to Think Like a 21st Century Economist* (White River Junction, VT: Chelsea Green, 2017). The one economics book everyone needs to read!

11 Ibid., p. 44. For example, the indicator for food shortfall is the percent of global population undernourished. The indicator for climate change overshoot is atmospheric carbon dioxide concentration, parts per million (ppm).

12   The Fairness Doctrine of the United States Federal
      Communications Commission (FCC), introduced in 1949, was
      a policy that required the holders of broadcast licenses both to
      present controversial issues of public importance and to do so
      in a manner that was honest, equitable and balanced. In 1987,
      the FCC abolished the fairness doctrine. https://en.wikipedia.
      org/wiki/FCC_fairness_doctrine

13   In 2019, Fox News was the top-rated cable network, averaging
      2.5 million viewers. https://en.wikipedia.org/wiki/Fox_News

14   Over two billion people use Facebook every month, making
      the network's News Feed the most viewed and most influential
      aspect of the news industry. https://en.wikipedia.org/wiki/
      News_Feed

15   A nod to Noam Chomsky, *Profit Over People: Neoliberalism &
      Global Order* (New York: Seven Stories Press, 1999)

16   Korten, *Agenda for a New Economy*

17   Ibid., pp. 209-218.

18   Piketty, *Capitalism and Ideology*, p. 972.

19   Ibid., p. 990.

20   Samuel Bowles and Herbert Gintis, *Democracy & Capitalism*
      (New York: Basic Books, 1986), p. 183.

21   Shoshana Zuboff, *The Age of Surveillance Capitalism* (New York:
      Public Affairs, 2019)

FURTHER READING

I described many important ideas in the main text as concisely as I could in order to sustain the book's flow and focus on a higher-level synthesis. This section highlights sources providing greater detail, depth, and nuance. These are the sources I relied upon most in writing this book.

Introduction

Naomi Klein, *This Changes Everything: Capitalism vs. The Climate* (New York: Simon & Schuster, 2014) – The title says it all! This book broke the ice and catalyzed the focus of the climate movement on how capitalism attacks life on Earth. It is loaded with good stories and incisive analysis. Klein's appeal for a new worldview inspired me and helped to give focus to *Which Future?* Beyond this global influence on the book, her views figure prominently in Part II, chapter six, under "Earth Does Not Belong to Humans."

Part I

Walter Truett Anderson, *Reality Isn't What It Used to Be* (New York: Harper & Row, 1990) – A brilliant, readable, comprehensive survey of the social construction of reality in the post-modern landscape as it was emerging. In this lively and penetrating book, Anderson weaves captivating stories of identity, belief systems, and worldviews into a coherent and fascinating tapestry.

Peter L. Berger and Thomas Luckmann, *The Social Construction of Reality: A Treatise in the Sociology of Knowledge* (New York: Doubleday & Company, 1966) – This book is the source of the sociological components of Part I. Here is where terms like reification, projection, institutionalization, and, above all, legitimation are defined, explained, and put into a larger theoretical framework. Though not an easy read, it is a profoundly insightful and enlightening one.

Jerome Bruner, *Acts of Meaning* (Cambridge, MA: Harvard University Press, 1990) – A true masterpiece, both personal and erudite, featuring detailed accounts of children internalizing their culture's folk psychology as they learn to speak its language. It is also a decisive argument for an interpretive, cultural psychology rather than the information-processing, computational agenda of prior decades. Though brief, this is a compelling book by a great cognitive psychologist.

Terrence W. Deacon, *The Symbolic Species: The Co-evolution of Language and the Brain* (New York: W.W. Norton, 1997) – A lengthy and challenging tome, and a feast for the intellect. Deacon's basic thesis about the discontinuity between human language and animal communication was persuasive to me, based on his extremely detailed and sophisticated analysis of the component issues. If this kind of seriously intellectual book is your cup of tea, you won't be disappointed.

Clifford Geertz, *The Interpretation of Cultures* (New York: Basic Books, 1973) – The "Bible" of cultural anthropology: a groundbreaking book as fresh today as it was 50 years ago. This book explores what culture means in terms of how to study and describe it. It offers riveting theory, analysis, and detailed observation intertwined expeditiously. It is endlessly fascinating; I can't imagine writing Part I without it.

Jonathan Haidt, *The Righteous Mind: Why Good People are Divided by Politics and Religion* (New York: Random House,

2012) – A justifiably popular book, included here despite my reservations about Haidt's political analysis, because he so thoroughly and brilliantly explains our ultimate emotional need to be validated as a good person, which plays such a crucial role in the self-fulfilling dynamics of belief systems.

Thomas S. Kuhn, *The Structure of Scientific Revolutions, Second Edition, Enlarged* (Chicago: University of Chicago Press, 1970; first edition 1962) – This is on the very short list of books that changed how I thought about everything. Using science history as a case study, Kuhn shows how what we take to be knowledge rests on social agreement, values, and shared exemplars. It is fundamental to understanding paradigms and paradigm shifts, and, moreover, the entire interplay of knowledge and authority that weaves through the social construction of reality.

Part II

Fritjof Capra and Pier Luigi Luisi, *The Systems View of Life: A Unifying Vision* (New York: Cambridge University Press, 2014) – This essential book expands on, integrates, and illuminates all the subjects I cover in chapters four and five, together with other important subjects beyond the scope of my book. Written primarily for undergraduates, it is both comprehensive and readable, and most highly recommended for inquisitive minds of all ages.

Peter Corning, *Synergistic Selection: How Cooperation Has Shaped Evolution and the Rise of Humankind* (Hackensack, N.J.: World Scientific, 2018) – Synergy and cooperation in evolution deserve more serious attention than my brief allusions in chapter five. This book rectifies that shortfall. Corning carries his brilliant, thorough, and quite readable analysis of synergy all the way from molecules through contemporary economics.

Antonio Damasio, *Self Comes to Mind: Constructing the Conscious Brain* (New York: Random House, 2010) – Damasio is a distinguished, world-class clinical neuroscience researcher, a sophisticated philosopher, a bold theoretician, and an oft-published author with the soul of a poet. With this book he became my go-to source for how the brain works, particularly the role of homeostasis and "biological value" in brain function. His theory of the evolution of the "autobiographical self" alone is worth the price of admission. This is a very readable and fascinating book.

Eva Jablonka and Marion J. Lamb, *Evolution in Four Dimensions: Genetic, Epigenetic, Behavioral, and Symbolic Variation in the History of Life, revised edition* (Cambridge, MA: M.I.T. Press, 2014) – This book provides a view of evolution that puts the "selfish gene" in its place. It is especially valuable for showing in detail how the logical scheme of genetic evolution applies in the same way to epigenesis, behavior, and symbolic (cultural) variation, all illustrated by the latest research studies. It is beautifully written and impressively argued.

Andrew H. Knoll, *A Brief History of Earth: Four Billion Years In Eight Chapters* (New York: HarperCollins, 2021) – An excellent book from which to grasp and appreciate the concept of Deep Time, which is manifest in our planet's entire geological history and in the amazing story of forms of life evolving in tandem with Earth's atmosphere over billions of years. It is engrossing and highly readable.

Donella H. Meadows, Dennis L. Meadows, and Jørgen Randers, *Beyond The Limits: Confronting Global Collapse, Envisioning a Sustainable Future* (Post Mills, VT: Chelsea Green, 1992) – Thirty years ago, these world-class authors used systems thinking and computer modeling to demonstrate conclusively the consequences of exponential growth for a finite world. This definitive and compelling book is specific and detailed, including a host of constructive suggestions and resources. Here we truly grapple with the nuts and bolts of "Humanity's Relationship to Nature."

William T. Powers, *Behavior: The Control of Perception* (Chicago: Aldine Publishing, 1973) – A unique and very important book which does a figure-ground reversal of common sense (behavior controls perception, not vice versa). I relied on Powers' cybernetic logic and analysis often in chapter five; it dovetails with the equally counterintuitive notion that the nervous system is closed to the environment. See notes seven and fifteen to chapter five ("Living Systems") for specific examples of Powers' thinking.

Ilya Prigogine and Isabelle Stengers, *Order Out of Chaos: Man's New Dialogue With Nature* (New York: Bantam, 1984) – Prigogine's Nobel Prize-winning work and theorizing about thermodynamics and complexity changed the way everyone understands nature at its deepest levels. For one thing, he demonstrated how "dissipative systems" are the physical basis of self-organization. This widely read book explains all this and goes deeper, making an incalculable contribution to science. (Chapter eight of Capra and Luisi [above] provides an excellent summary of these subjects.)

David Sloan Wilson, *This View of Life: Completing the Darwinian Revolution* (New York: Pantheon Books, 2019) – An engaging and thorough master class on how evolutionary theory applies to culture as much as it does to genes. A core source on multilevel selection (Part II, chapter five and Part III, chapter eight) and cultural evolution (Part III, chapter eleven). Moreover, the book is full of constructive thoughts on policy and politics, reflecting Wilson's years of activist social experiments to develop practical uses of evolutionary theory in daily life. Superb popular writing about science and society.

PART III

Janine M. Beynus, *Biomimicry: Innovation Inspired by Nature* (New York: William Morrow, 1997) – A significant piece of the sustainability puzzle. Nature as a model, as a measure, and as a mentor. Engagingly written, this book shows how to solve human problems sustainably by studying how nature does it. It is full of detailed stories about growing food, harnessing energy, manufacturing, healing, and conducting business. This book evolved under Beynus's leadership into the Biomimicry Institute, a thriving community with a great online presence.

Anthony Biglan, *The Nurture Effect* (Oakland, CA: New Harbinger, 2015) – My chapter ten on "Humanist Values and Principles" devotes a few paragraphs to the foundational importance of caring and nurturing environments for human well-being. This book was a core source. Biglan is a big thinker and activist as well as a major behavioral scientist. His book is full of wisdom and practical solutions to important social issues. It deserves a wide audience.

Lester R. Brown, *Plan B 3.0: Mobilizing to Save Civilization* (New York: W.W. Norton, 2008) – This book is the definitive source for what it will take for humanity to live sustainably, comprehensively summarizing Brown's decades of work with the Earth Policy Institute. It contains detailed facts and analysis of the most important global environmental and economic problems, as well as an intelligent set of constructive responses to them. It is essential reading.

Riane Eisler and Douglas P. Fry, *Nurturing Our Humanity: How Domination and Partnership Shape Our Brains, Lives, and Future* (New York: Oxford University Press, 2019) – I love this book! We share the same "biosocial" paradigm of explanation. The book is mindfully written, carefully documented, and smoldering with moral passion just under the surface of its judicious analyses. It is comprehensive and mainstream in presentation yet radical in argument and implications. I cite it throughout Part III. It is an ideal source for further depth and nuance.

David C. Korten, *Agenda For A New Economy: From Phantom Wealth to Real Wealth (2nd ed.)* (San Francisco: Barrett-Koehler, 2010) – A brilliant and essential book. Korten is both a sophisticated economist and a committed humanist who proposes replacing the entire Wall Street enterprise with a decentralized "Main Street" economic system. It is a great read, full of practical, concrete policy and political proposals, and a core source for Part III.

Thomas Piketty, *Capitalism and Ideology* (Cambridge, MA: Belknap/Harvard University Press, 2020) – A lengthy and extensive work without peer by a world-renowned French economist who studies historical data. With a unique blend of scholarship, humanity, and incisive expression, Piketty reviews historical "inequality regimes" through the lens of the ideology used to justify them. In the end, he advocates a new "participatory socialism" based on equality, education, and the sharing of knowledge and power. A contemporary masterpiece.

Kate Raworth, *Doughnut Economics: 7 Ways to Think Like a 21st Century Economist* (White River Junction, VT: Chelsea Green, 2017) – A revolutionary paradigm for economists in a world committed to sustainability. I feature her "doughnut" metaphor in chapter eleven and hope it becomes to the 21st century what the solar system was to the 20th—something every child learns about in elementary school. The remainder of the book gently introduces the main themes of ecology and social justice to budding economists and the rest of us.

Robert B. Reich, *The Common Good* (New York: Alfred A. Knopf, 2018) – It is too easy to assume we all know what is meant by "the common good." Here, the former Secretary of Labor masterfully lays out in specific terms what it means for our country in its present political moment. The book is not only a welcome expansion of the moral arguments I make in chapters eight and ten, but also a playbook for liberals and progressives going forward.

Michael J. Sandel, *The Tyranny of Merit: Can We Find the Common Good?* (New York: Farrar, Straus and Giroux, 2020) – A priceless contribution to the public interest. Sandel's critique reveals the hubris a meritocracy generates among the winners and the harsh judgment it imposes on those left behind. In search of the common good today, he argues for a broad, democratic "equality of condition" (very much like what I propose in chapters ten and eleven), in which the dignity of all work and solidarity around the project of democracy maintain the bonds of the common good. This is moral philosophy of the first order.

Robert M. Sapolsky, *Behave: The Biology of Humans at Our Best and Worst* (New York: Penguin Books, 2017) – The author, both a primatologist and a neuroscientist, has produced over 700 pages of immense readability, a cross-disciplinary survey of our glands, genes, and childhoods, and a tour de force of synthesis and explanation. But, above all, it's Sapolsky's genius to have organized the first five chapters by the timing of explanatory events rather than by classes of behavior, demonstrating the overriding lesson that there are always multiple explanations for any significant behavior. This is an entertaining, profound, and outstanding book!

Frans de Waal, *The Bonobo And The Atheist: In Search Of Humanism Among The Primates* (New York: W.W. Norton, 2013) – Everything de Waal writes is thoughtful, interesting, and very readable. In this book, he argues that the roots of human morality are biological, and, as they say, he had me from the very beginning. Interweaving primate stories with philosophical analysis, he strongly influenced my overall disposition toward a naturalist morality, as is most explicitly credited in chapter eight. This is a major contribution to natural humanism.

INDEX

ABOUT THE AUTHOR

David Greene is an independent scholar passionate about contributing to human welfare and justice. An instinctively holistic thinker and Stanford PhD in social psychology, he has enjoyed careers in academia, software development, and K-12 education policy research and evaluation. Along the way, he has conducted significant research at Amherst College, the University of Pennsylvania, Stanford University, Carnegie Mellon University, and SRI International, and has conducted funder-initiated evaluations in the Chicago and Los Angeles public schools and for the Lawrence Hall of Science.

To follow and contribute to continuing conversations about natural humanism, please visit the author and book's website at **www.WhichFutureBook.com**.

www.ingramcontent.com/pod-product-compliance
Lightning Source LLC
Chambersburg PA
CBHW022048020426
42335CB00012B/591